INTRODUCING ISSUES WITH OPPOSING VIEWPOINTS

Child Abuse

William Dudley, *Book Editor*

Christine Nasso, *Publisher*
Elizabeth Des Chenes, *Managing Editor*

Garfie

GREENHAVEN PRESS
An imprint of Thomson Gale, a part of The Thomson Corporation

Detroit • New York • San Francisco • New Haven, Conn. • Waterville, Maine • London

Picture Credits:
Cover photo: photos.com; Maury Aaseng, 13, 19, 24, 38, 40, 47, 67, 78, 84, 90, 104; AP Images, 10, 14, 17, 22, 28, 34, 39, 42, 45, 52, 58, 62, 68, 74, 77, 80, 83, 88, 95, 102

LIBRARY OF CONGRESS CATALOGING-IN-PUBLICATION DATA

Child abuse / William Dudley, book editor.
    p. cm. — (Introducing issues with opposing viewpoints)
Includes bibliographical references and index.
ISBN-13: 978-0-7377-3803-2 (hardcover)
1. Child abuse—United States. 2. Child sexual abuse—United States. I. Dudley, William, 1964–
    HV6626.52.C535 2008
    362.760973—dc22

                                                                2007038335

ISBN-10: 0-7377-3803-0

Printed in the United States of America

Contents

Foreword

Indulging in a wide spectrum of ideas, beliefs, and perspectives is a critical cornerstone of democracy. After all, it is often debates over differences of opinion, such as whether to legalize abortion, how to treat prisoners, or when to enact the death penalty, that shape our society and drive it forward. Such diversity of thought is frequently regarded as the hallmark of a healthy and civilized culture. As the Reverend Clifford Schutjer of the First Congregational Church in Mansfield, Ohio, declared in a 2001 sermon, "Surrounding oneself with only like-minded people, restricting what we listen to or read only to what we find agreeable is irresponsible. Refusing to entertain doubts once we make up our minds is a subtle but deadly form of arrogance." With this advice in mind, Introducing Issues with Opposing Viewpoints books aim to open readers' minds to the critically divergent views that comprise our world's most important debates.

Introducing Issues with Opposing Viewpoints simplifies for students the enormous and often overwhelming mass of material now available via print and electronic media. Collected in every volume is an array of opinions that captures the essence of a particular controversy or topic. Introducing Issues with Opposing Viewpoints books embody the spirit of nineteenth-century journalist Charles A. Dana's axiom: "Fight for your opinions, but do not believe that they contain the whole truth, or the only truth." Absorbing such contrasting opinions teaches students to analyze the strength of an argument and compare it to its opposition. From this process readers can inform and strengthen their own opinions, or be exposed to new information that will change their minds. Introducing Issues with Opposing Viewpoints is a mosaic of different voices. The authors are statesmen, pundits, academics, journalists, corporations, and ordinary people who have felt compelled to share their experiences and ideas in a public forum. Their words have been collected from newspapers, journals, books, speeches, interviews, and the Internet, the fastest growing body of opinionated material in the world.

Introducing Issues with Opposing Viewpoints shares many of the well-known features of its critically acclaimed parent series, Opposing Viewpoints. The articles are presented in a pro/con format, allowing readers to absorb divergent perspectives side by side. Active reading questions preface each viewpoint, requiring the student to approach the material thoughtfully and carefully. Useful charts, graphs, and cartoons supplement each article. A thorough introduction provides readers with crucial background on an issue. An annotated bibliography points the reader toward articles, books, and Web sites that contain additional information on the topic. An appendix of organizations to contact contains a wide variety of charities, nonprofit organizations, political groups, and private enterprises that each hold a position on the issue at hand. Finally, a comprehensive index allows readers to locate content quickly and efficiently.

Introducing Issues with Opposing Viewpoints is also significantly different from Opposing Viewpoints. As the series title implies, its presentation will help introduce students to the concept of opposing viewpoints, and learn to use this material to aid in critical writing and debate. The series' four-color, accessible format makes the books attractive and inviting to readers of all levels. In addition, each viewpoint has been carefully edited to maximize a reader's understanding of the content. Short but thorough viewpoints capture the essence of an argument. A substantial, thought-provoking essay question placed at the end of each viewpoint asks the student to further investigate the issues raised in the viewpoint, compare and contrast two authors' arguments, or consider how one might go about forming an opinion on the topic at hand. Each viewpoint contains sidebars that include at-a-glance information and handy statistics. A Facts About section located in the back of the book further supplies students with relevant facts and figures.

Following in the tradition of the Opposing Viewpoints series, Greenhaven Press continues to provide readers with invaluable exposure to the controversial issues that shape our world. As John Stuart Mill once wrote: "The only way in which a human being can make some approach to knowing the whole of a subject is by hearing what can be said about it by persons of every variety of opinion and studying all modes in which it can be looked at by every character of mind. No wise man ever acquired his wisdom in any mode but this." It is to this principle that Introducing Issues with Opposing Viewpoints books are dedicated.

Introduction

"Child abuse does not discriminate. It spans all racial, gender, socio-economic and demographic boundaries."

—American Humane Association, *Child Abuse*

Michael and Iana Shaw, a young married couple in Reno, Nevada, were the parents of two children—a boy just under two years old and a girl just under one. In 2007 social workers found these children severely malnourished and rushed them to a local hospital. The girl weighed only ten pounds and had a mouth infection and severe dehydration. Her hair was matted with cat urine and had to be shaved. The boy was having difficulties walking because of retarded muscle development. According to Kelli Ann Viloria, a local prosecutor, the children were starving because the parents were too occupied playing with their newly purchased television and computer system. "They had food; they just chose not to give it to their kids because they were too busy playing video games."[1]

This case is an extreme example of child neglect—the failure to provide life's basic necessities. Child neglect is a form of child abuse; others include beating or physical abuse, sexual abuse, and emotional abuse. The U.S. government defines the term *child abuse* as actions that result in "death, serious physical or emotional harm, sexual abuse or exploitation, . . . [or] an imminent risk of serious harm"[2] to children. Of the estimated three million cases of child abuse and neglect that happen in the United States each year, an estimated fourteen hundred result in child fatalities. But it is often only the fatalities or stories like the Shaw children's that receive media coverage and focus society's attention on child abuse. Such stories also place a spotlight on the social institutions that are supposed to prevent abuse in cases where parents, or other primary caregivers, pose a danger to children.

Two distinct social agencies deal with child abuse. One is the criminal justice system. In cases of serious abuse, the abusers may find themselves arrested by the police, tried for criminal acts (such as assault, rape, or homicide), and sentenced to prison if found guilty. In the

Shaw case, the two parents pleaded guilty to two counts each of child neglect and face prison terms of up to twelve years.

Most initial reports of child abuse, however, are not investigated by the police but rather by someone in the local child protective services department. For these workers, their decision often focuses on what to do with the victim, not what to do with the abuser. They have the authority to legally take children away from their parents or family caregivers, if necessary, and place them in foster care. (The Shaw children were placed into foster care and were doing well and gaining weight a month after their hospitalization, according to Viloria.)

Law enforcement and child protective services broadly represent two social strategies dealing with the problems of child abuse. One strategy focuses on the safety of the children, treats child abusers simply as criminals, and calls for the child's immediate removal from environments where abuse is suspected. An aggressive approach along these lines might have removed the Shaw children from their parents at the first allegations or signs of neglect, saving them from near death. Such thinking is also behind the acts of many communities to shelter children from stranger abuse, such as laws preventing convicted sex offenders from hanging around parks, schools, and other places frequented by children.

But there is another school of thought that argues that many parents and caregivers who abuse or neglect their children should not be treated as criminals but rather as victims themselves. Studies of child abuse have shown that many perpetrators were child abuse victims themselves and developed warped notions of how to discipline or treat children. Other studies have shown that child abuse is often linked with substance abuse, stress caused by poverty, and other factors. Perhaps the Shaw children could have been saved from hardship had their parents received mental health counseling dealing with their video addiction or had parenting classes available for them.

If such is indeed the case—that child abuse could be prevented by helping potential child abusers resolve their own problems—then treating child abuse as primarily a manner of criminal justice has two possible drawbacks. One is that law enforcement does not get involved until after child abuse has been committed; it does little to prevent child abuse in the first place. The second drawback is that an approach emphasizing law enforcement may deter families and others from reporting abuse if they believe it will get the parents into prison or into legal trouble. The temptation will be greater to sweep child abuse situations "under the rug" and to fail to get parents necessary counseling or other help that might prevent abuse.

The relative merits of these two general approaches to fighting child abuse is just one of several debates surrounding this issue. Other debates revolve around the difficult choices faced by both law enforcement and welfare personnel in deciding at what point families should be torn apart and children taken away from their parents. *Introducing Issues with Opposing Viewpoints: Child Abuse* presents diverse opinions and arguments on these and other topics pertaining to child abuse. The viewpoints presented illustrate that while no one disagrees about the necessity of preventing and punishing child abuse, disputes do exist about how society can best protect America's children.

Notes

1. Associated Press, "Internet Obsession Blamed for Neglect," July 14, 2007.
2. U.S. Department of Health and Human Services, Administration for Children and Families, *Child Maltreatment 2005.* Washington, DC: U.S. Government Printing Office, 2007.

Chapter 1

How Serious Is the Problem of Child Abuse?

This cage was used to keep an abused child under wraps by its parents.

Child Abuse Is a Serious National Problem

"Child abuse is a hideous, widespread and chronic problem across the country."

Bob Herbert

Bob Herbert is a columnist for the *New York Times*. In the following viewpoint he describes several horrible deaths suffered by children at the hands of abusive parents or stepparents. These cases, he argues, are simply the most shocking examples of the serious problem of child abuse in America. There exists a crisis both in the extent of child abuse and neglect and in the failure of state child protective services to keep children from harm, he contends.

AS YOU READ, CONSIDER THE FOLLOWING QUESTIONS:

1. What anecdote about child abuse does Herbert use to begin his article?
2. How many children die from child abuse or neglect, according to the author?
3. Children most likely to be abused come from what social and economic class, according to Herbert?

Two little boys—toddlers in Yonkers—died horrible deaths last July [2005] when they were left alone in a bathroom with scalding water running in the tub. The water overflowed and flooded the room. The children, in agony, were unable to escape as the water burned and blistered their feet and ankles and kept on rising. One of the boys struggled to save himself by standing on his toes, but to no avail.

Authorities said that when the boys were found, they were lying face up in the water on the bathroom floor, their bodies all but completely scorched. They had burned to death.

The boys—one was nearly three years old and the other 20 months—had been left in the bathroom (which had a damaged door that was difficult to open) by David Maldonado, the live-in boyfriend of the boys' mother. Police said he was the father of one of the children.

The two adults had taken heroin. While the children suffered and died, the grown-ups, according to the authorities, were lying in bed, lost in a deep drug-fueled sleep. Both have pleaded guilty in connection with the deaths, and have been imprisoned.

A Chronic and Widespread Problem

I've been reading (and sometimes writing) stories like this for many years. Every few months or so, some horrifying child abuse case elbows its way onto the front pages, and there is a general outcry: How could this have happened? Where were the caseworkers? Lock up the monsters who did this! Let's investigate and reform the child welfare system.

And then the story subsides and we behave as if this murderous abuse of helpless children trapped in the torture chambers of their own homes has somehow subsided with it. But child abuse is a hideous, widespread and chronic problem across the country. And despite the sensational cases that periodically grab the headlines, it doesn't get nearly enough attention.

What some adults do to the children in their care can seem like behavior left over from the Inquisition. According to the U.S.

FAST FACT

Four children die each day due to abuse or neglect, according to the U.S. Advisory Board on Child Abuse and Neglect.

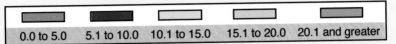

Child Abuse Victims per 1,000 Children

0.0 to 5.0	5.1 to 10.0	10.1 to 15.0	15.1 to 20.0	20.1 and greater

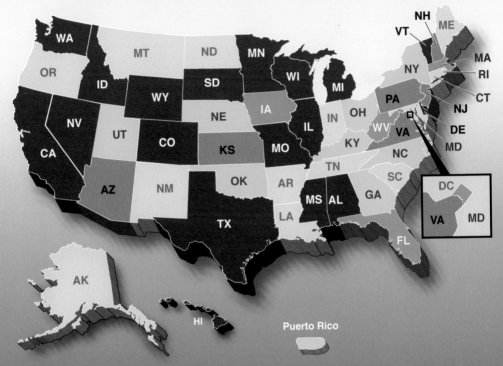

Source: U.S. Department of Health and Human Services, Administration for Children and Families, *Child Maltreatment 2005* (Washington, DC: U.S. Government Printing Office, 2007).

Department of Health and Human Services, nearly 1,500 children died from abuse or neglect in 2003, the latest year for which reasonably reliable statistics are available [as of March 2006]. That's four children every day, and that estimate is probably low. Record-keeping in some states is notoriously haphazard.

Authorities in Michigan reported the heartbreaking case of a 7-year-old, Ricky Holland, who begged his school nurse not to send him home to his adoptive parents. "Let me stay in school," he pleaded.

He was later beaten to death with a hammer, prosecutors said, and his bloody body was dragged away in a garbage bag. His parents were charged with his death.

Former New York mayor Rudolph Giuliani attends a wake for a six-year-old child who was allegedly beaten to death by her mother.

The deaths, as horrible as they are, don't begin to convey the enormity of the problem. In 2003, authorities were alerted to nearly three million cases of youngsters who were alleged to have been abused or neglected, and confirmed a million of them. The number of cases that never come to light is, of course, anybody's guess.

What's remarkable to me is that we've been hearing about this enormously tragic problem for so long, decades, and yet the reaction to each sickening case that makes it into the media spotlight is shock. How many times are we going to be shocked before serious steps are taken to alleviate the terrible suffering and prevent the horrible deaths of as many of these children as we can?

What We Know About Abuse

We know some things about child abuse and neglect. We know that there is a profound connection between child abuse and substance abuse, for example. We know that abuse and neglect are more likely to occur in households where money is in short supply, especially if the caregivers are unemployed. A crisis in the home heightens the chances that a child will be abused. And adults who were abused as children are more likely than others to be abusers themselves.

Child-abuse prevention programs are wholly inadequate, and child protective services, while varying in quality from state to state, are in many instances overwhelmed and largely unaccountable. The child protection system has broken down—or was never up and running at all—in state after state after state.

"There are no consequences to violating policy," said Marcia Robinson Lowry, executive director of the advocacy group Children's Rights. "There are no consequences to violating the law."

The kids who are most frequently the victims of abuse are from the lower economic classes. They are not from families that make a habit of voting. There is no real incentive for government officials to make the protection of these kids a priority.

They couldn't be more alone. They are no one's natural constituency.

EVALUATING THE AUTHOR'S ARGUMENTS:

Herbert asserts that public attention to the problem of child abuse is not sufficient. What evidence does he provide to back his claim? Do you believe his proffered evidence sufficiently supports his conclusion? Why or why not?

Child Abuse in America Is Declining

St. Louis Post-Dispatch

> *"Rates of physical and sexual abuse plummeted over the last decade."*

The following viewpoint is taken from a 2007 editorial by the *St. Louis Post-Dispatch*, a daily newspaper serving St. Louis, Missouri, and the surrounding region. The writers note that, according to statistics kept nationally and in the St. Louis region, rates of child physical and sexual abuse have been significantly declining. The authors provide several possible reasons for these positive trends, including greater public awareness of child abuse and increased staffing in police and child welfare departments. They conclude that child abuse remains a problem about which all people should remain vigilant.

AS YOU READ, CONSIDER THE FOLLOWING QUESTIONS:

1. How much did sexual assaults against teens decline between 1993 and 2004, according to the authors?
2. What form of child victimization has not followed the general trend of decline?
3. What steps do the authors recommend to maintain progress on the child abuse issue?

In the past decade, the incidence of child abuse—locally and nationally—has declined sharply.

Rates of physical and sexual abuse plummeted over the last decade, with substantiated sex abuse cases plunging 51 percent overall since 1991, according to federal statistics. Before that, child sexual abuse had increased steadily for at least 15 years. Physical abuse cases have dropped 46 percent overall from their peak in 1992. And in 2005, the most recent year for which federal data were available, rates of child physical and sexual abuse also fell slightly from the prior year.

Encouraging Statistics

Sexual assaults against teenagers fell 67 percent between 1993 and 2004, according to data from the National Crime Victimization Survey. And even greater declines were seen in assaults against teens by strangers, the same survey found. Other crimes against young people also decreased from 1993 to 2004: Aggravated assaults against young people ages 12 to 17 were down 74 percent, and juvenile homicides fell 50 percent—an even larger decline than for adult murder victims.

Paper cutouts of children from one state (measured as one cutout per county) help to show the decline in child abuse.

Data from government surveys that track child welfare mirror the abuse trends. Delinquency, running away from home and teen suicide, often linked to physical and sexual abuse, also fell.

It's all good news. National statistics like these are something to celebrate. Locally [St. Louis, Missouri] the news also is positive. Child abuse is declining in Illinois and Missouri, according to experts here. "We are consistently going down each year in the number of substantiated cases of child abuse," said Ana Margarita Compain-Romero, spokeswoman for the Missouri Department of Social Services.

Child Neglect

But one area of child victimization has not shown the same encouraging decline: child neglect. For reasons that are unclear, the number of substantiated child neglect cases rose 14 percent between 1990 and 2003. Child neglect accounts for about two-thirds of the 3 million reports made to child protective services nationwide each year. Neglect can be as damaging as abuse, causing mental and physical health problems and contributing to juvenile delinquency and adult criminal behavior, according to Dr. Howard Dubowitz, professor of pediatrics and director of the Center for Child Protection at the University of Maryland School of Medicine.

FAST FACT

Less than 1 percent of child abuse cases involve murder.

Although the downward trends are encouraging, child abuse and neglect in the United States still are far too common, and much higher than in other wealthy nations. About one in four girls and one in six boys are sexually abused by the time they reach 18, according to Jerry Dunn, executive director of Children's Advocacy Services of Greater St. Louis. Her agency, which works closely with law enforcement agencies to investigate abuse and neglect allegations, interviewed about 300 children last year [2006].

Researchers suggest a number of reasons for these positive trends: improvements in the economy; more child protective workers and police abuse investigators; greater public awareness of child abuse; better parenting and the increased use of psychiatric medications.

Violent Crimes Against Teenagers

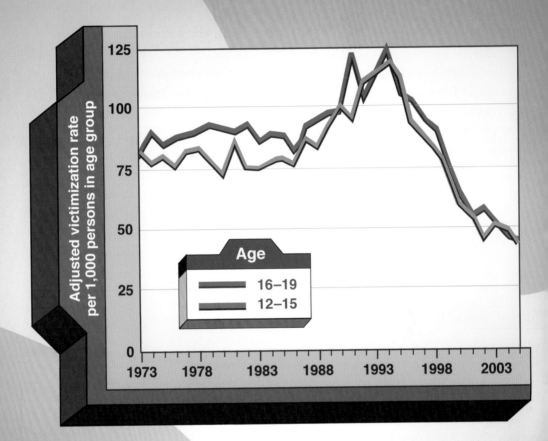

This chart shows rates of violent crimes against young people. Violent crimes included are homicide, rape, robbery, and both simple and aggravated assault.

For victims ages 12–15, the rate per 1,000 population began at 81.8 in 1973 and fell to 76.4 in 1976. Then the rates climbed to 83.7 in 1978, before falling to 72.5 in 1980. Then it increased to a high of 118.6 in 1994, before decreasing to a low of 44.0 in 2005.

For victims ages 16–19, the rate per 1,000 population began at 81.7 in 1973 and increased, reaching a high of 94.4 in 1982. The rate then dropped, reaching 80.8 in 1986, before increasing to 123.9 in 1994. Then it fell to a low of 44.3 in 2005.

Source: Bureau of Justice Statistics, 2006. www.ojp.usdoj.gov/bjs/.

Risking Complacency

But with such dramatic overall improvements comes a risk of complacency.

"What I don't want to have happen is for the community to let its guard down," Ms. Dunn said.

Nowhere is that more important than in cyberspace, where internet pornography—including child pornography—is ubiquitous and adults misrepresent themselves as teens in order to lure victims into sexually compromising situations.

To reduce the incidence of abuse and neglect even further, experts recommend a continued investment in parenting education, drug and mental health treatment, public awareness campaigns and social norms that set a low tolerance for the mistreatment of children. Reducing poverty and unemployment, ensuring access to contraception and offering support services to stressed families also would help. Eliminating child abuse and neglect is not just the job of social workers and police.

Protecting our children is everyone's business.

EVALUATING THE AUTHORS' ARGUMENTS:

The authors use statistics from government sources to buttress their argument that child abuse is declining. Is this a valid use of statistics, in your view? Why or why not?

Child Abuse Perpetrated by Women Is a Serious Problem

Carey Roberts

"Women are the most common abusers of children."

Carey Roberts argues in the following viewpoint that child abuse by women poses a bigger problem than child abuse by men. He complains that the media, the general public, and the criminal justice system treat female child abusers more leniently than male offenders. Such a double standard, he argues, endangers children. Roberts is a journalist and writer whose work has appeared in the *Washington Times, Intellectual Conservative,* and other publications.

AS YOU READ, CONSIDER THE FOLLOWING QUESTIONS:

1. What examples of child abuse by females does Roberts describe?
2. What percentage of child abuse and neglect cases are perpetrated by women, according to the author?
3. What excuses do women use to avoid criminal punishment, according to Roberts?

Carey Roberts, "Double-Standard Treatment for Child Abusers," ifeminists.com, January 18, 2006. Reproduced by permission.

Heather Thomas of Fairfax, VA, was arrested last week [in January 2006] in the shaking death of her 6-day-old granddaughter. On Christmas Day Valerie Kennedy held her son in a tub of scalding water as punishment, causing his death. A few days later Genevieve Silva was arrested in Oklahoma on child rape charges for luring a high school student to run away from home.

Linda Aube was charged with first-degree murder and first-degree child abuse when she confessed to punishing her son for splashing in the bathtub by holding him underwater.

Women Abusers

Chances are you didn't read about these incidents in your local newspaper. Because when a man commits abuse, it seems the story is splashed all over the front page. But when the perpetrator is a member of the fairer sex, the story is relegated to the bottom of the Police Report on page C9.

Each year the federal Administration for Children and Families surveys child protective service (CPS) agencies around the country to spot the latest trends in child abuse. And according to the National Child Abuse and Neglect Data System, women are the most common abusers of children.

FAST FACT

A 1996 study showed that nearly 80 percent of fatal maltreatment cases were attributed to women.

In 2003, females, usually mothers, represented 58% of perpetrators of child abuse and neglect, with men composing the remaining cases. In that same year an estimated 1,500 children died of abuse or neglect. In 31% of those cases, the perpetrator was the mother acting alone, compared to 18% of fathers acting alone.

Dumpster Babies

Then there's the scandal of Dumpster babies. In 1998, 105 newborn infants were discovered abandoned in public places. One-third of those babies were found dead.

In a civilized society that makes adoption services widely-available, that practice should have been condemned as unconscionable and wrong. But instead of prosecuting the abandoners, we accommodated to the societal imperative to provide choices to women no matter the moral consequences. So we passed laws to establish "safe havens."

Under New York law, mothers can now anonymously drop off their infants up to five days old. But if she later has second thoughts, not to worry. She can come back and reclaim the child up to 15 months later.

That satisfaction-guaranteed-or-your-money-back offer might work at a Macy's handbag sale, but that's not how a moral society treats its most vulnerable members.

Age and Sex of Child Abuse Perpetrators

Age	Men Number	Men Percent	Women Number	Women Percent	Total Number	Total Percent
< 20	22,853	6.4	19,787	4.1	42,640	5.1
20–29	100,195	28.3	200,053	41.2	300,248	35.7
30–39	128,784	36.3	179,447	36.9	308,231	36.7
40–49	75,391	21.3	66,973	13.8	142,364	16.9
> 49	27,117	7.7	19,811	4.1	46,928	5.6
Total	345,340	100.0	486,071	100.0	840,411	100.0
Weighted percent		42.2		57.8		100.0

Source: U.S. Department of Health and Human Services, Administration for Children and Families, *Child Maltreatment 2005* (Washington, DC: U.S. Government Printing Office, 2007).

Patricia Pearson has written a blockbuster book called, *When She Was Bad: Violent Women and the Myth of Innocence.* Pearson documents repeated examples of violent women who draw their Get-Out-of-Jail-Free card by claiming PMS, battered woman's syndrome, or postpartum depression.

Remember Andrea Yates, who admitted to drowning her five boys in a bathtub? Of course the National Organization for Women rushed to her defense, claiming that postpartum blues justified the serial murder. . . .

Then there's the problem of women, usually female teachers, who seduce and deflower teenage boys. Look how the media sanitizes the issue. Reporters trivialize the incident using clinical phrases such as "sexual contact," or worse, envelop the story in a snickering "didn't-he-get-lucky" tone.

I once knew a teenage boy who was raped by his older sister's girlfriend during a holiday visit to his parent's home. Ten years later, he was still devastated by the incident. Of course he never reported the assault, no one would have taken him seriously.

A Double Standard

When these cases go to trial, the double standard persists. As CNN's Nancy Grace plaintively asks, "Why is it when a man rapes a little girl, he goes to jail, but when a woman rapes a boy, she had a breakdown?"

And shame on reporters who use limp clichés to excuse the inexcusable. Like the story about a New Orleans mom who stuffed her 3-month-old son in the clothes dryer and hit the On button. This was the feeble explanation that the *Times-Picayune* offered in its December 8 [2005] edition: "Murder Suspect 'Was Trying her Best.'"

That condescending headline brings to mind the Solomonic words of columnist Kathryn Jean Lopez: "There are mental-health issues in many of these cases, obviously, but regardless, a society can and must say loud and clear: 'That's wrong. That's evil. That can never happen again.'"

To which I say, "Amen."

In radio talk shows and internet bulletin boards around the nation, Americans' ire has reached the boiling point over female child abusers who are treated with reverential deference by the media and our legal system.

As long as we tolerate this gender double-standard, the problem will fester and grow. And our children will continue to be at risk.

EVALUATING THE AUTHOR'S ARGUMENTS:

What connection does the author make between child abuse and "safe haven" laws? Do you agree or disagree with his expressed opposition to such laws? Explain your answer.

Child Abuse by Siblings Is a Serious Problem

Kyla Boyse

> "*Research shows that violence between siblings is quite common.*"

The following viewpoint is excerpted from a fact sheet on sibling abuse that uses a question-and-answer format to examine the problem. The primary author, Kyla Boyse, argues that physical, emotional, and sexual abuse between young siblings is a prevalent problem that might be even more common than child abuse inflicted by adults. She describes several risk factors for sibling abuse and steps that parents and others should take if they witness such behavior. Boyse is a registered nurse with the University of Michigan Health System.

AS YOU READ, CONSIDER THE FOLLOWING QUESTIONS:
1. According to Boyse, why do many parents fail to recognize sibling abuse?
2. How common is abuse between siblings, according to the author?
3. What does Boyse contend are some of the lasting effects of child abuse by siblings?

W*hat is sibling abuse?* Sibling abuse is the physical, emotional or sexual abuse of one sibling by another. The physical abuse can range from relatively mild forms of aggression occurring between siblings, such as pushing and shoving, to extremely violent behavior such as the use of weapons.

Often parents don't recognize the abuse for what it is. Typically, parents and society *expect* fights and other physical forms of aggression to occur among siblings. Because of this, sibling abuse often is not seen as a problem until serious injuries occur. Another factor is that in some cases, siblings may switch back and forth between the roles of abuser and victim.

Besides the immediate dangers of sibling abuse, the abuse can cause all kinds of problems on into adulthood. Being abused by a sibling can really mess up a person's life.

How common is sibling abuse? Research shows that violence between siblings is quite common. In fact, it is probably even more common than child abuse (by parents) or spouse abuse. The most violent members of American families are the children. It has been estimated that three children in 100 are *dangerously violent* toward a brother or sister. Likewise, many researchers have estimated *sibling incest* to be much more common than parent-child incest. It seems that when abusive acts occur between siblings, they are often not perceived as abuse.

FAST FACT

Brother-sister incest may be five times more common than father-daughter incest.

Recognizing Sibling Abuse
How do I identify abuse? What is the difference between sibling abuse and sibling rivalry? At times, all siblings squabble and call each other mean names, and some young siblings will "play doctor." But here is the difference between typical sibling behavior and abuse: If one child is always the victim and the other child is always the aggressor, it is an abusive situation.

Some possible signs of sibling abuse are:
• One child always avoids their sibling
• A child has changes in behavior, sleep patterns, eating habits, or has nightmares

Sibling abuse, such as physical, emotional, or sexual abuse, is a prevalent problem that may go unnoticed by adults.

- A child acts out abuse in play
- A child acts out sexually in inappropriate ways . . .

Areas of Concern

What are some of the risk factors for sibling abuse? Much more research needs to be done to find out how and why sibling abuse happens. Some risk factors are

- Parents are not around much at home
- Parents are not very involved in their children's lives, or are emotionally unavailable to them
- Parents accept sibling rivalry as part of family life, rather than working to minimize it
- Parents do not stop children when they are violent (they may assume it was accidental, part of a two-way fight or normal horseplay)
- Parents increase competition among children by:
  - playing favorites
  - comparing children
  - labeling or type-casting children (even casting kids in positive roles is harmful)

- Parents have not taught children about sexuality and about personal safety
- Parents and children are in denial that there is a problem
- Children have inappropriate family roles, for example, they are burdened with too much care-taking responsibility for a younger sibling
- Children are exposed to violence
  - in their family (domestic violence)
  - in the media
  - among their peers or in their neighborhoods (for example, bullying)
- Children have been sexually abused or witnessed sexual abuse
- Children have access to pornography . . .

How to Handle Sibling Abuse

What should I do if there's abuse going on between my kids? When one sibling hits, bites, or physically tortures a brother or sister, the normal rivalry has become abuse. You can't let this dangerous behavior continue. Here's what to do:

- Whenever violence occurs between children, separate them.
- After a cooling off period, bring all the kids involved into a family meeting.
- Gather information on facts and feelings.
- State the problem as you understand it.
- Help the kids work together to set a positive goal. For example, they will separate themselves and take time to cool off when they start arguing.
- Brainstorm many possible solutions to the problem, and ways to reach the goal.
- Talk together about the list of solutions and pick the ones that are most acceptable to everyone.
- Write up a contract together that states the rights and responsibilities of each child. Include a list of expected behavior, and consequences for breaking the code of conduct.
- Make sure you don't ignore, blame, or punish the victim.
- Make your expectations and the family rules very clear.
- Continue to carefully monitor your kids' interactions in the future.
- Help your kids learn how to manage their anger.

If problems continue or violent behavior is extreme your family should get professional help.

Long-Term Effects

Can sibling relationships have lasting effects into adulthood? In the last few years, more research has been done on the lasting effects of early experiences with sisters and brothers. Siblings can have strong, sometimes long-lasting effects on one another's emotional development as adults.

Research indicates that long-term effects of sibling abuse can include:
- Depression, anxiety, and low self-esteem
- Inability to trust, relationship difficulties
- Alcohol and drug addiction
- Eating disorders

Even less extreme sibling rivalry during childhood can create insecurity and poor self-image in adulthood. Sibling conflict does not have to be physically violent to take a long-lasting emotional toll. Emotional abuse, which includes teasing, name-calling, and isolation, can also do long-term damage.

EVALUATING THE AUTHOR'S ARGUMENTS:

One of the questions Boyse answers is how to distinguish between sibling abuse and normal sibling rivalry. How would you answer that question? Is it different from or similar to Boyse's answer? Explain.

Internet Child Sexual Predators Are a Prevalent Problem

"No child is safe from . . . men who use the Internet in an attempt to realize their worst fantasies."

Greg Abbott

Greg Abbott is the attorney general for the state of Texas. He previously served as a justice on the Texas Supreme Court. One of Abbott's initiatives as the state's chief law enforcement official was to establish the Cyber Crimes Unit to investigate and arrest people who use the Internet to abuse or prey upon children. The following viewpoint is taken from 2006 testimony before Congress on the problem of child sexual abuse and the Internet. Abbott describes his work in Texas and argues that computers have empowered child abusers to seek out and victimize more children. Society should do more to protect children from Internet predators, he concludes.

AS YOU READ, CONSIDER THE FOLLOWING QUESTIONS:
1. What examples of Internet-empowered child abuse does Abbott describe?
2. How many teenagers use the Internet, according to the author?
3. How does the Internet create opportunities for child predators, according to the author?

Greg Abbott, testimony before the House Committee on Energy and Commerce, House Subcommittee on Telecommunications and the Internet, July 11, 2006.

The dangers to children created by social networking websites and chat rooms are very real. The Texas experience is both illustrative and alarming. Three years ago [in 2003], we created a Cyber Crimes Unit in the Office of the Attorney General of Texas. One of its primary missions was to find, arrest and convict child predators who use the Internet to stalk their prey. The unit's nationally recognized success is tragic evidence of the risk children face when using chat rooms or social networking websites. Our Cyber Crimes Unit has investigators who log onto chat rooms that are used by teenagers. Sometimes they log on to social networking sites like MySpace. The investigators typically assume the identity of a teenage girl, usually around the age of 13 or 14. Not long after they log on and assume an under-age identity, they are barraged with aggressive and vulgar language that is uninvited. All too often, the offensive Internet "chat" turns into action. The predator sets a time, date and location to sexually assault what he believes to be a 13- or 14-year-old girl. On more than 80 occasions, the predator has shown up at the location of his choosing to act out on his criminal intent. The location is sometimes a motel, sometimes an apartment, sometimes a parking lot, sometimes other places. It is not uncommon for the predator to bring things like condoms, alcohol, even a bed. Each of those 80+ occasions has resulted in an arrest of the child predator by the Texas Attorney General's Office.

Arresting Child Predators

As an example, we recently arrested a 50-year-old man after he showed up at a Central Texas restaurant to meet what he thought was a 14-year-old girl. This predator had been talking with the girl—who in reality was one of our Cyber Crimes investigators—in an online chat room. He even stopped on his way to the meeting and bought some wine coolers to give the girl. And not long ago, we arrested a 52-year-old university professor at a bus station in McAllen, Texas, where he was waiting for what he thought was a 13-year-old girl he met online. He even bought the would-be teenager a bus ticket so she could travel from miles away to meet him. The 80th arrest was particularly notable. It was the arrest of 27-year-old John David Payne, who had been chatting with what he thought was a 13-year-old girl he met on MySpace. In reality, the graphic sexual conversations he was having were with a Texas Attorney General investigator. What makes his case particularly frightening—although sadly not unusual—is that, at the time of his arrest, Mr. Payne was out on bail from an arrest that occurred six months prior. In fact, at the time of his most recent arrest, he was already under indictment for online solicitation of a minor. In other words, while he was out on bond awaiting trial for illegal Internet solicitation of a minor, he was back on the Internet, trolling for his next victim. These child predators are dangerous and incorrigible, and children simply cannot be safe with the current landscape of cyberspace chat rooms and social networking sites. Unfortunately, not all of the people chatting with predators are undercover officers, and not all of the predators are caught in stings. Real children are real victims of real predators. Recently, a 14-year-old girl from Central Texas was raped by a man she chatted with on a social networking site. This is just one of the most recent examples, examples that are repeated around the country with increasing frequency.

The Need for Safeguards

As we hold this hearing today [July 11, 2006], millions of teenagers are chatting online, posting personal information on a profile page, talking to other teens on social networking sites, and meeting people in chat rooms. Before we leave here today, countless of those teens will have innocently chatted with someone they didn't know. And, before we leave today, some of those unknown chatters will turn out to be predators who have just located their next target. Clearly, safeguards are needed at schools and libraries—as well as in our homes—if we are to protect our children against these predators. Such safeguards are the kinds of protections that Americans have come to expect. Streets, neighborhoods and playgrounds are essential to our

It is important for adults to frequently scan Internet chat rooms for sexual predators to protect children from such harm.

daily lives and are part of the American social and economic fabric. Nevertheless, we must police our streets, neighborhoods and play-grounds to ensure their safety. Similarly, the Internet superhighway and social network sites are vital to our modern day economy, and they provide an effective platform for the exchange of ideas, infor-mation and commerce. They also have developed into virtual neigh-borhoods where people can simply socialize. But, these modern-day neighborhoods and playgrounds are proving just as susceptible to criminals and predators as their traditional counterparts, if not more so. . . . Computer literacy and Internet access are necessities, not luxuries. And without question they have made our lives better. But the anonymity of the Internet has created opportunities for child predators and child pornographers, giving them cover to act on their perversions. It turns out that the Internet, for all of its benefits and all of its conveniences, is still a pretty dangerous place. It would not be an exaggeration to say that no child is safe from the unwanted advances of chat room predators, men who use the Internet in an attempt to realize their worst fantasies.

EVALUATING THE AUTHOR'S ARGUMENTS:

Abbott argues that the Internet forms virtual neighborhoods that, just like real neighborhoods, need police protection. Do you believe his analogy is a good one? Why or why not?

The Threat of Online Sexual Abuse Is Overblown

Pete Reilly

"You'd never know [that child abuse is decreasing] from the hype the media is giving the cases of online related sexual abuse that they can trace back to MySpace or Facebook."

Pete Reilly argues in the following viewpoint that parental fears of computer-assisted child sexual abuse by strangers is being stoked by media reports and is unduly hampering the use of promising information technologies. He argues that child abuse is dramatically declining, contrary to impressions one may get from the media, and that most child abuse occurs within the family, unaffected by school policies or the Internet. Parents and educators should be prudent about young people's computer use, but they should not make policies out of fear, he argues. Reilly is a teacher and the leader of several organizations that work to help schools utilize computers in education.

AS YOU READ, CONSIDER THE FOLLOWING QUESTIONS:

1. What actions have schools taken to protect students from computer-assisted child abuse, according to Reilly?

Pete Reilly, "The Facts About Online Sex Abuse and Schools," *The Pulse, District Administration blogs,* January 6, 2007. Reproduced by permission.

2. What does Reilly suggest educators could do to decrease child and sexual abuse?
3. What percentage of reported online child abuse occurred outside the home, according to Reilly?

Since 9/11 the mantra of "national security" has justified just about any action the power structure in Washington has wished to undertake. In educational circles the magical mantra has been "student safety." The fear of online predators has been used to curtail, restrict, and prohibit the use of some of the most promising online educational technology tools.

In order to avoid an incident where a student is exposed to an online predator, "cyber-bullied" by classmates, or exposed to inappropriate material from the school's Internet connection, educational leaders are routinely restricting the use of blogs, podcasts, e-mail, instant messaging, wikis, and other promising Web 2.0 tools. We've even decided to ban student photos from our school web pages.

How justified are our fears?

There are some statistics that raise alarm bells [such as] Four (4) percent of all youth Internet users in 2005 said online solicitors asked them for nude or sexually explicit photographs of themselves. . . .

Putting Fears into Perspective

Maintaining the safety of the children in their charge is a major part of the social bargain between parents and schools. Parents, who drop off their most treasured possessions at the school's doorstep, expect them to be returned safely, and more knowledgeable than when they left them.

There is another set of "facts" that might put these fears into perspective.

A good place to start is to look at the steadily decreasing Child Sexual Abuse trends:

All forms of child abuse, not just sexual abuse, are undergoing a dramatic decline. Of course, you'd never know this from the hype the media is giving the cases of online related sexual abuse that they can trace back to MySpace or Facebook.

Estimated Number of Substantiated Cases of Sexual Abuse in the United States, 1990–2000

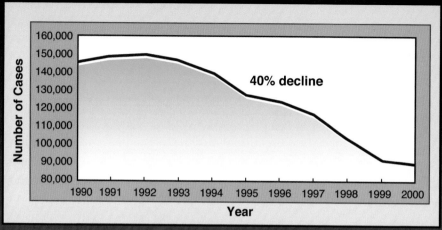

Source: Author's analysis of data from 1990–2000, National Child Abuse and Neglect Data System (NCANDS) reports (U.S. Department of Health and Human Services, 1992–2002).

Perpetrators by Relationship to Victims, 2004

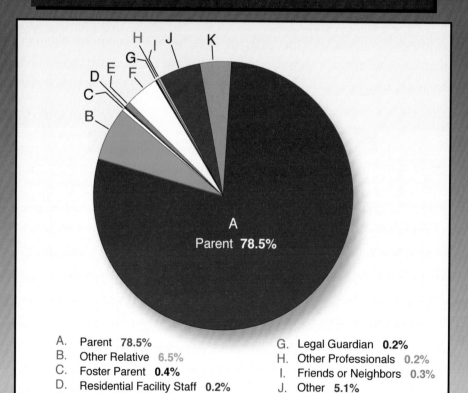

A. Parent **78.5%**
B. Other Relative 6.5%
C. Foster Parent **0.4%**
D. Residential Facility Staff **0.2%**
E. Child-Day-Care Provider 0.7%
F. Unmarried Partner of Parent **4.1%**

G. Legal Guardian **0.2%**
H. Other Professionals 0.2%
I. Friends or Neighbors 0.3%
J. Other **5.1%**
K. Unknown or Missing 3.9%

Source: http://preilly.files.wordpress.com/2006/12/perpetrator-3.jpg.

Not all teenagers use the Internet irresponsibly.

The picture painted by the media leaves the impression that child abuse and sexual abuse are increasing and that our children are under siege from online strangers using the Internet to snare their victims. [The pie chart on page 38] puts some perspective on the threat from strangers, online, or not.

The amazing and sad statistic that is so often overlooked and rarely discussed is that 95% of Child Abuse and Sexual Abuse is perpetrated by family members. 79% of perpetrators are parents. Other relatives accounted for 7% and unmarried partners of parents and "other" accounted for 4% and 5% of abuse.

FAST FACT

According to a 2004 Pew survey, 21 million teens use the Internet, and half of them say they go online every day.

If we want to decrease child and sexual abuse, our efforts would be far more effective if we focused our attention on the families of our students rather than the few sensationalized online incidents that the media trumpets so loudly.

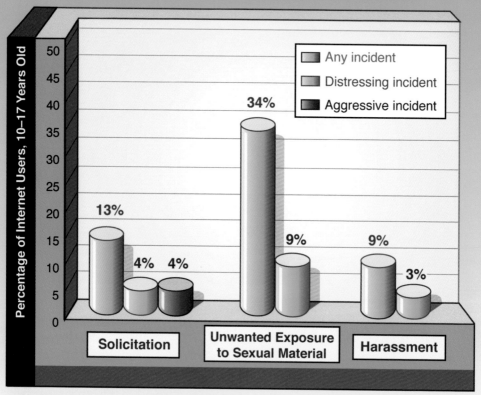

Percentage of Teens Surveyed Reporting Internet-Related Problems

Percentage of Internet Users, 10–17 Years Old

Legend:
- Any incident
- Distressing incident
- Aggressive incident

Solicitation: 13%, 4%, 4%

Unwanted Exposure to Sexual Material: 34%, 9%

Harassment: 9%, 3%

Source: National Center for Missing and Exploited Children, 2006.

A great way for schools to reduce the incidence of child and sexual abuse is to train their staffs to identify the warning signs. Although educators report more abuse than any other sector of society, incidents continue to be severely under-reported. . . .

Of the five percent (5%) of abuse perpetrated by those other than family members, the Internet is involved in only a small percentage. Definitive statistics on the prevalence of online cases is difficult to document.

It is also important to point out that 79% of reported online abuse occurred at the victim's home, 9% happened at school, 5% happened at friend's homes, and 5% happened at other places, including the library. When we slice the "less than five percent pie" into these smaller pieces, the risk gets much, much smaller. Of course, statistics aren't going to matter much if you are the parent of a child who has had an online incident, or the leader of a school that has experienced one.

A "Zero Risk" Approach?

The question is, "Are we going to take a 'zero risk' approach to using technology and the tools of the Web?"

We don't take a "zero risk" approach with our sports programs where the chance of injury, paralysis, and, in rare cases, death, is always present. We don't take that approach with field trips where students travel to museums and historical sites in locations where they might be touched by crime. We don't take that approach with recess on our playgrounds, or transporting our kids to and from school.

We can never eliminate all risk; but there are ways to maximize our students' safety while using these incredibly powerful tools. Each tool needs to be analyzed individually to ascertain its benefits and the specific risks it might present. From there, thoughtful people can find solutions to the student safety issues that may arise.

As educational leaders we need to be safety conscious. We need to be prudent, reasonable; but we won't live in fear and we won't act from fear.

It is by opening doors, not closing them that we create new possibilities for our children and new futures for ourselves.

EVALUATING THE AUTHOR'S ARGUMENTS:

What do you make of the author's argument that "zero risk" is impossible, and that parents accept this fact in field trips or sports and should do the same for computer activities? When can the quest for "zero risk" go too far, in your opinion?

Chapter 2

How Can Child Abuse Be Prevented?

Special events are hosted to start off National Child Abuse Prevention Month across the United States such as the "Candle of Hope" lighting in Merced, California, in 2003.

Laws Against Spanking Can Reduce Child Abuse

Emily Bazelon

"Allowing for 'reasonable' spanking gives parents a lot of leeway to cause pain."

In January 2007 the California state legislature briefly considered a proposal that would outlaw all corporal punishment of children under the age of four. The idea sparked a national debate on spanking and the law. In the following viewpoint, Emily Bazelon argues that such a ban could reduce child abuse. She maintains that current laws, which prohibit child abuse but exempt spanking that is "reasonable," are confusing because there is no clear definition as to what "reasonable" is, giving parents room to cause harm. Furthermore, Bazelon asserts, a state law prohibiting spanking would make it easier for police and prosecutors to bring charges against parents who physically abuse their children. Bazelon is a senior editor at *Slate*.

AS YOU READ, CONSIDER THE FOLLOWING QUESTIONS:

1. What does Bazelon say is the purpose of Assemblywoman Lieber's proposal?

2. What have been the effects of the 1979 law against corporal
   punishment in Sweden?
3. According to psychologist Diana Baumrind, why shouldn't we
   fight over the "occasional spank"?

S ally Lieber, the California assemblywoman who proposed a ban
on spanking last week [January 2007] must be sorry she ever
opened her mouth. Before Lieber could introduce her bill, a poll
showed that only 23 percent of respondents supported it. Some pedi-
atricians disparaged the idea of outlawing spanking, and her fellow
politicians called her crazy. Anyone with the slightest libertarian streak
seems to believe that outlawing corporal punishment is silly. More
government intrusion, and for what—to spare kids a few swats? Or,
if you're pro-spanking, a spanking ban represents a sinister effort to
take a crucial disciplinary tool out of the hands of good mothers and
fathers—and to encourage the sort of permissive parenting that turns
kids ratty and rotten.

The Purpose of Lieber's Proposal

Why, though, are we so eager to retain the right to hit our kids? Lieber's
ban would apply only to children under the age of 4. Little kids may be
the most infuriating; they are also the most vulnerable. And if you think
that most spanking takes place in a fit of temper—and that banning it
would gradually lead more parents to restrain themselves—then the idea
of a hard-and-fast rule against it starts to seem not so ridiculous.

The purpose of Lieber's proposal isn't to send parents to jail, or children to foster care, because of a firm smack. Rather, it would make it
easier for prosecutors to bring charges for instances of corporal punishment that they think are tantamount to child abuse. Currently,
California law (and the law of other states) allows for spanking that
is reasonable, age-appropriate, and does not carry a risk of serious
injury. That forces judges to referee what's reasonable and what's not.
How do they tell? Often, they may resort to looking for signs of injury.
If a smack leaves a bruise or causes a fracture, it's illegal. If not, bombs
away. In other words, allowing for "reasonable" spanking gives parents a lot of leeway to cause pain.

The United Nations Reports on Violence Against Children

Who should we worry about more: The well-intentioned parent who smacks a child's bottom and gets hauled off to court, or the kid who keeps getting pounded because the cops can't find a bruise? [A 2006] U.N. report on violence against children argues that "The de minimis principle—that the law does not concern itself with trivial matters, will keep minor assaults on children out of court, just as it does almost all minor assaults between adults." The U.N. Committee on the Rights of the Child has been urging countries to ban corporal punishment since 1996. The idea is that by making it illegal to hit your kids, countries will make hurting them socially unacceptable.

The United Nations has a lot of converting to do in this part of the world. Its report cites a survey showing that 84 percent of Americans believe that it's "sometimes necessary to discipline a child with a good hard spanking." On this front, we are in the company of the Koreans, 90 percent of whom reported thinking that corporal punishment is "necessary." On the other side of the spanking map are 19 countries that have banned spanking and three others that have partially banned it.

Laws prohibiting the marketing or use of devices specifically for hitting or whipping children are being legislated across the United States.

The Effects of Sweden's Law

The grandmother of the bunch is Sweden, which passed a law against corporal punishment in 1979. The effects of that ban are cited by advocates on both sides of the spanking debate. Parents almost universally used corporal punishment on Swedish children born in the 1950s; the numbers dropped to 14 percent for kids born in the late 1980s, and only 8 percent of parents reported physically punishing their kids in 2000. Plus, only one child in Sweden died as the result of physical abuse by a parent between 1980 and 1996. Those statistics suggest that making spanking illegal contributes to making it less prevalent and also to making kids safer. On the other hand, reports to police of child abuse soared in the decades after the spanking ban, as did the incidence of juvenile violence. Did reports rise because frustrated, spanking-barred parents lashed out against their kids in other ways, or because the law made people more aware of child abuse? The latter is what occurred in the United States when reports of abuse spiked following the enactment of child-protective laws in the 1970s. Is the rise in kids beating on each other evidence of undisciplined, unruly child mobs, or the result of other unrelated forces? The data don't tell us, so take your pick.

FAST FACT

In May 2007 New Zealand became the eighteenth country—and the first English-speaking country—to ban all corporal punishment of children.

Further Studies

A similar split exists in the American social-science literature. In a 2000 article in the *Clinical Child and Family Psychology Review*, Dr. Robert Larzelere (who approves of spanking if it's "conditional" and not abusive) reviewed 38 studies and found that spanking posed no harm to kids under the age of 7, and reduced misbehavior when deployed alongside milder punishments like scolding and timeouts. By contrast, a 2002 article in *Psychology Bulletin* by Dr. Elizabeth Gershoff (not a spanking fan) reviewed 88 studies and found an association between corporal punishment and a higher level of childhood aggression and a greater risk of physical abuse.

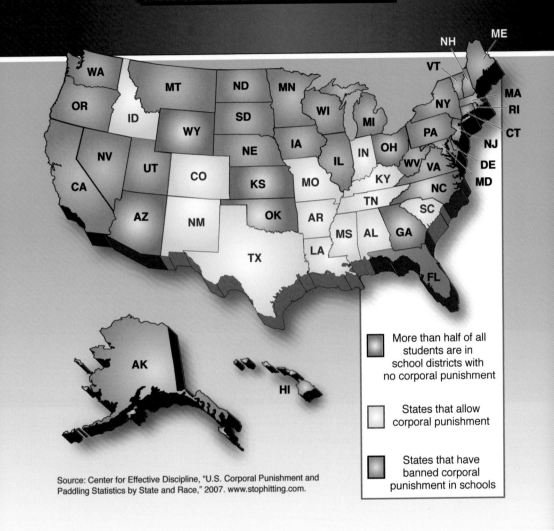

States Banning Corporal Punishment in Schools

More than half of all students are in school districts with no corporal punishment

States that allow corporal punishment

States that have banned corporal punishment in schools

Source: Center for Effective Discipline, "U.S. Corporal Punishment and Paddling Statistics by State and Race," 2007. www.stophitting.com.

This is the sort of research impasse that leaves advocates free to argue what they will—and parents without much guidance. But one study stands out: An effort by University of California at Berkeley psychologist Diana Baumrind to tease out the effects of occasional spanking compared to frequent spanking and no spanking at all. Baumrind tracked about 100 white, middle-class families in the East Bay area of northern California from 1968 to 1980. The children who were hit frequently were more likely to be maladjusted. The ones who were occasionally spanked had slightly higher misbehavior scores than those who were not spanked at all. But this difference largely disappeared when Baumrind accounted for the children's poor behavior at a younger age. In other words, the kids who acted out as toddlers and preschoolers were more likely to act out later, whether they were spanked occasionally or never. Lots of spanking was bad for kids. A little didn't seem to matter.

Baumrind concluded that it is "*reliance* on physical punishment, not whether it is used at all, that is associated with harm to the child." The italics are mine. While Baumrind's evidence undercuts the abolitionist position, it doesn't justify spanking as a regular punishment. In addition, Baumrind draws a telling distinction between "impulsive and reactive" spanking and punishments that require "some restraint and forethought." In my experience as a very occasional (once or twice) spanker, impulsivity was what hitting my kid was all about. I know that I'm supposed to spank my sons more in sorrow than in anger. But does that really describe most parents, especially occasional spankers, when they raise their hand to their children? More often, I think, we strike kids when we're mad—enraged, in fact. Baumrind's findings suggest that occasional spankers don't need to worry about this much. I hope she's right. But her numbers are small: Only three children in her study weren't spanked at all. That's a tiny control group.

The Occasional Spank

Baumrind argues that if the social-science research doesn't support an outright ban on spanking, then we shouldn't fight over the occasional spank, because it diverts attention from the larger problems of serious abuse and neglect. "Professional advice that categorically rejects any and all use of a disciplinary practice favored and considered functional by parents is more likely to alienate than educate them," she argues. The extremely negative reaction to Lieber's proposed ban is her best proof.

It's always difficult and awkward—and arguably misguided—to use the law as a tool for changing attitudes. In the case of corporal punishment, though, I'm not sure we'd be crazy to try. A hard-and-fast rule like Sweden's would infuriate and frustrate some perfectly loving parents. It would also make it easier for police and prosecutors to go after the really bad ones. The state would have more power over parents. But then parents have near infinite amounts of power over their kids.

EVALUATING THE AUTHOR'S ARGUMENTS:

Bazelon argues that America should in fact outlaw spanking, yet cites that only 23 percent of poll respondents supported the ban. Do you agree with Bazelon or with the majority who think no such ban should be instated? Explain your answer.

Spanking Laws Are Not an Effective Method of Child Abuse Prevention

"It's hard to see how . . . putting mom or dad in jail for a spanking could be even remotely in a toddler's interest."

Debra J. Saunders

Spanking and other forms of corporal punishment are against the law in many countries but are legal in several U.S. states. In January 2007 a California state legislator proposed outlawing spanking in that state. In the following viewpoint, Debra J. Saunders argues that most spanking does not injure children—and that hitting a child hard enough to cause injury is already against the law. The proposed spanking ban, she contends, is an invasion of privacy and is more about imposing certain parenting philosophies than about child safety. Saunders is a columnist for the *San Francisco Chronicle*.

AS YOU READ, CONSIDER THE FOLLOWING QUESTIONS:
1. What are the penalties for spanking under the proposed California law that Saunders criticizes?
2. What examples of real child abuse does Saunders describe in contrast to spanking?
3. What question did California governor Arnold Schwarzenegger have about the proposed ban, according to Saunders?

Assemblywoman Sally Lieber, D-Mountain View, has announced that she will introduce a bill [in January 2007] to make it a crime to spank children who are 3 years old or younger, punishable by up to a year in jail or a $1,000 fine. If this zany idea were to become law, California could be the place where the nanny state meets the authoritarian state.

It is more than ironic that a politician who wants to make it illegal for parents to apply their flat hands to their babies' bare bottoms is more than happy to allow the heavy hand of the law to yank parents from their homes and place them behind bars for disciplining their children in the way which they see fit and does not injure a child.

"I think we ought to have a law against beating children," Lieber told *The [San Francisco] Chronicle*. . . .

A Misguided Proposal

That's the problem. California does have laws against beating children. But in this politically correct atmosphere, do-gooders believe it is their right to pass laws that expand definitions beyond reason so that a spanking is a beating—even when it isn't.

FAST FACT

Polls have found that roughly two-thirds of American parents approve of spanking.

In effect, this is what Lieber is saying in proposing such a law: I know how to raise your kids and I am going to make it illegal for other parents to discipline their children in a way I do not like. If you don't do it my way, you can go to jail.

That's not how Lieber sees it, of course. She told me, "I haven't heard any convincing arguments as to why anyone would want to swat a 6-month-old or 1-year-old." As Lieber sees it, spanking is "not effective," children under 3 "don't understand it." And: spanking trains children "in violence and domination, even when it's moderate."

While Lieber may believe that she is trying to protect children, it's hard to see how a big fine or putting mom or dad in jail for a spanking could be even remotely in a toddler's interest.

Problems with Enforcement

Let me be clear. I am not defending spanking. Like Lieber, I don't think spanking is effective and there are better ways to discipline children.

I just happen to believe that California cops have their hands full dealing with adults who beat, torture and or otherwise abuse children. Take

Lawmakers trying to tell parents they cannot discipline their child by spanking is believed to be overkill and a potential invasion of privacy.

the case of Oakland's Chazarus Hill Sr., 27, who beat his 3-year-old son Chazarus "Cha Cha" Hill Jr. to death in 2003 after the poor boy wet his bed and made mistakes recognizing flash cards. Cha Cha had been beaten repeatedly before his father killed him—and I want police to concentrate on finding and going after adults like Hill. California law rightly gives law enforcement the tools to prosecute such parents—and it is on such cases, of bodily injury, that law should and must focus. Indeed, state law mandates that teachers, health-care professionals and cops report suspected child abuse to the proper authorities.

Lieber mentioned the Hill case over the phone—which is wrongheaded because Hill was beating his son with deadly weapons—switches and belts—for weeks before he killed him.

Joseph D. McNamara, a retired police chief of San Jose and now a research fellow at Stanford's Hoover Institution, told me that if he were a beat cop, he would be "horrified" at the prospect of enforcing a spanking ban. Such a law would put police in "everyone's living rooms" where they would have to regulate parenting.

Or as Gov. Arnold Schwarzenegger so aptly put it when first told about the proposed law, "How do you enforce that?"

Parents Know Difference Between Spanking and Abuse

McNamara told me he never spanked his children, but he could conceive of instances in which good parents might choose to do so. Say a parent repeatedly tells a young child not to run into the street, or not to talk to strangers or to stop hurting a younger sibling—and words alone have not worked.

In such cases, parents—not a Sacramento lawmaker—know what best to do. And while Lieber told me she wants to draw a line that makes physical discipline a "black and white" issue, California parents have been dealing with shades of gray since before Lieber was in diapers. Parents are not stupid, they know the difference between beating and spanking, and they do not need her to draw the line for them.

What's next—McNamara wondered—a law against grabbing your kid by the arm? Pass such laws, he added, and you'll see a state in which "parents are afraid to discipline the child." As if that would be good for California families.

Lieber's response is that wife-beating once was off-limits to law enforcement, but in this enlightened age, the law does come between a man's fist and his wife's face. Again, she fails to distinguish between beating and spanking. Just as some people choose not to distinguish between physical and verbal abuse.

Lieber explained, "Things have changed. Now we tell parents what to do and what not to do." The state makes adults use car seats for small children and there are laws to keep them away from lead-based paint.

Except spanking doesn't cause physical harm, as car accidents and lead paint can. And if spanking does injure children, it is illegal. This is more about philosophy than safety—and California lawmakers don't have a right to mandate how parents think about raising their own kids. Those who want the government to stay out of the bedroom should not want it in the nursery or at the kitchen table either. [*Editor's note:* Lieber withdrew her proposed spanking ban in February 2007 after failing to gain enough votes to pass the measure.]

EVALUATING THE AUTHOR'S ARGUMENTS:

Saunders says she is not personally in favor of spanking. Do you think this admission strengthens or weakens her argument against making spanking a criminal act? Why or why not?

Federal Laws Regulating Social Networking Web Sites Can Prevent Sexual Exploitation

"The dangers our children are exposed to by these [social networking] sites are clear and compelling."

Michael G. Fitzpatrick

Michael G. Fitzpatrick is a Republican politician who was elected to Congress in 2004. In 2006 he introduced the Deleting Online Predators Act, requiring schools and libraries to restrict young people from social networking Web sites and chat rooms. The following viewpoint is taken from testimony before a Senate committee in which he defends his proposed legislation and argues that social networking sites such as MySpace.com increase the risks of children being approached and possibly victimized by sexual predators. The bill was passed by the House but not the Senate; Fitzpatrick himself was narrowly defeated in his bid for reelection in 2006.

Michael G. Fitzpatrick, testimony before the House Committee on Energy and Commerce, Subcommittee on Oversight and Investigations, *Sexual Exploitation of Children over the Internet: How the State of New Jersey Is Combating Child Predators on the Internet,* June 10, 2006.

AS YOU READ, CONSIDER THE FOLLOWING QUESTIONS:
1. How popular are social networking sites, according to Fitzpatrick?
2. Why are social networking sites dangerous for young people, according to the author?
3. What steps would Fitzpatrick's proposed bill take to protect children from online predators?

As the father of six children, I know very well the challenges technology poses to our families. In a world that moves at a dizzying pace, being a father gets harder all the time. Monitoring our children's use of emerging technologies is a huge task and the Internet remains the focus of many parent's concerns.

The technological breakthrough of the World Wide Web has been enormously beneficial to society. The Internet has brought communities across the globe closer together through instant communication. It has enabled an unfiltered free-flow of thought, ideas, and opinion. The Internet has opened a window to the world right at our fingertips. However, this window opens both ways. The freedom to connect to the world anywhere at anytime brings with it the threat of unscrupulous predators and criminals who mask their activities with the anonymity the Internet provides to its users. And among its many applications, one of the most worrying developments of late has been the growth in what are known as "social networking sites."

Social Networking Sites

Social networking sites like MySpace, Friendster, and Facebook have literally exploded in popularity in just a few short years. MySpace alone has almost 90 million users and ranks as the sixth most popular English language website and the eighth most popular site *in the world.*

Anyone can use these sites—companies and colleges, teachers and students, young and old all make use of networking sites to connect with people electronically to share pictures, information, course work, and common interests. These sites have torn down the geographical divide that once prevented long distance social relationships from forming, allowing instant communication and connections to take place and a virtual second life to take hold for its users.

For adults, these sites are fairly benign. For children, they open the door to many dangers including online bullying and exposure to child predators that have turned the Internet into their own virtual hunting ground. I became personally aware of the danger the Internet can pose after my 16-year-old daughter began using the social networking site MySpace.com. I quickly realized that while my daughter thought she was only chatting with her friends, other people, some with criminal intent, could be looking in.

Although age limits exist on many of these sites, there is almost no enforcement of these rules. Frequently, children under the age of 16—the cut off age for a profile on MySpace—simply lie about their age and fake being 16, 18 or even older. Predators also use this anonymity to their advantage by profiling themselves as teenagers to more easily identify and navigate the profiles of their prey.

Grave Dangers

The dangers our children are exposed to by these sites are clear and compelling. According to a study conducted by the National Center for Missing and Exploited Children (NCMEC), in 1998 there were 3,267 tips reporting child pornography. Since then, the number has risen by over 3,000 percent to an astounding 106,119 tips in 2004. The Department of Justice recognizes child pornography as a precursor for pedophiles and [it] is often linked to online predators. According to Attorney General [Alberto] Gonzales, one in five children has been approached sexually on the Internet. *One in five.* Worse still, a survey conducted by the Crimes Against Children Research Center found that less than one in four children told their parents

FAST FACT

As of July 2007 MySpace.com had removed 29,000 profiles of registered sex offenders from its network, out of its total of 180 million profiles.

about the sexual solicitation they received. MySpace, which is self regulated, has removed an estimated 200,000 objectionable profiles since it began operating in 2003. And while it is difficult to predict the exact number of total predators on the Internet at any one time, the Federal

The FBI and America Online have worked together to create a TipLine to stop Internet child predators.

Bureau of Investigation (FBI) estimates that there are more than 2,400 active child sexual exploitation investigations under way at any given time.

This problem is finally gaining the public's attention. Look closely at local and national news stories and you will undoubtedly see a story of a crime linked to social networking sites. Recently, national news reports have focused on the case of Katherine R. Lester, a 16-year-old Michigan honors student who fled to Israel with hopes of meeting a 25-year-old man she met on MySpace. Two months ago [April 2006], in my own congressional district, a 25-year-old man, Shawn Little, was arrested for posing as a teenager online to solicit a 14-year-old boy. Little's communications with the child resulted in a sexual encounter. And NBC's *Dateline* program has brought the threat of online predators to the televisions of millions of Americans through their acclaimed, but disturbing, "To Catch a Predator" series. While these high-profile cases make a splash on the headlines, how many other, less publicized cases of child exploitation go unnoticed?

The Deleting Online Predators Act

While these stories have pressured many social networking sites to take action to improve their safety protocols, like MySpace recently has done, these changes fall short of real reform. That is why I introduced the Deleting Online Predators Act.

Parents have the ability to screen their children's Internet access at home. But this protection ends when their child leaves for school or the library. My legislation would require schools and libraries to monitor the Internet activities of minors and implement technology to protect children from accessing:

1. Commercial networking sites like MySpace.com and chat rooms which allow children to be preyed upon by individuals seeking to do harm to our children; and
2. Visual depictions that are obscene or child pornography. . . .

In addition, my Bill would require the Federal Communications Commission to establish an advisory board to review and report commercial social networking sites like MySpace.com and chat rooms that have been shown to allow sexual predators easy access to personal information of, and contact with, children.

Make no mistake; child predation on the Internet is a growing problem. Predators will look for any way to talk to children online whether through sites like MySpace, instant messaging, or even online games. The best defense against these people is to educate parents and children of the dangers that come along with the Internet and by limiting access to certain sites during the school day.

EVALUATING THE AUTHOR'S ARGUMENTS:

Does Fitzpatrick's descriptions of social networking sites and their dangers correspond with your experience, if any, with these sites? Explain.

Viewpoint
4

Federal Laws Targeting Social Networking Web Sites Are Harmful

"To clamp down on a bunch of new networking sites really doesn't do anything' to stop sexual predators."

Wade Roush

In 2006 Congress debated a law—the Deleting Online Predators Act (DOPA)—that would restrict the access of students to social networking Web sites and chat rooms on school and library computers. Supporters of DOPA argued that such restrictions were necessary to protect children from online sexual predators. In the following viewpoint, Wade Roush presents several reasons why many educators and others opposed the proposed law, which did not pass. He argues that such federal regulation would do very little to protect children and would harm many by depriving them of the educational benefits of the Internet. Roush is a science writer and former editor for *Technology Review*.

Wade Roush, "The Moral Panic over Social-Networking Sites," TechnologyReview.com, August 6, 2006. Reproduced by permission.

AS YOU READ, CONSIDER THE FOLLOWING QUESTIONS:
1. What political considerations lay behind DOPA, according to its critics?
2. How might low-income students be especially harmed by federal laws restricting Internet access, according to Roush?
3. How might teens react if social networking Web sites were restricted, according to Roush?

The social-networking site MySpace has 95 million registered users. If it were a country, it would be the 12th largest in the world (ranking between Mexico and the Philippines). But under a bill designed to combat sexual predators on the Internet, MySpace and similar sites would become countries that young people can't visit—at least not using computers at schools or libraries.

The Deleting Online Predators Act (DOPA), introduced in the U.S. House of Representatives in May by Michael Fitzpatrick (R-PA), was passed by a vote of 410 to 15 on July 26 [2006]. It requires, with few exemptions, that facilities receiving federal aid block minors from accessing commercial social-networking sites and chat rooms, where they might encounter adults seeking sexual contact.

A Political Stunt?

The bill has now moved on to the Senate. [*Editor's note:* The bill was defeated in the Senate.] Critics from the worlds of educational technology and media studies say they're alarmed that the legislation has advanced this far. They warn that it would do little to stop sexual predators, but would deprive youth from poor areas of their only access to the online communities that are an increasingly critical part of teen culture. To these critics, the act is an election-year stunt designed to make any member of Congress who opposes it look "soft" on sexual predators.

It's a "monumentally ill-considered piece of legislation" that "by any rational measure" should never have left the House, says Henry Jenkins, professor of literature and director of the Comparative Media Studies Program at MIT [Massachusetts Institute of Technology].

Children, such as these first-graders, may be hindered by lawmakers' attempts to keep them safe from Internet predators.

Jenkins believes the act plays on parents' lack of understanding, and their resulting fears, about their kids' activities on the Internet. "But the price of standing up to that fear may be too high for liberal Democrats," he says.

If the Senate approves a similar bill and the legislation reaches President [George W.] Bush's desk, the price to young people will be even higher, say Jenkins and other critics. "If it would actually prevent predation, I would be fine with it," says Danah Boyd, a PhD candidate in the School of Information Management Sciences at the University of California, Berkeley, who is considered one of the leading scholarly authorities on social-networking sites. "But it's not going to help at all. Out of 300,000 child abductions every year, only 12 are by strangers. This is just going to stifle the social-networking industry and completely segment youth around economic status."

The impact on youth from economically disadvantaged families is what Jenkins worries about most. "Already, you have a gap between kids who have 10 minutes of Internet access a day at the public library and kids who have 24-hour-a-day access at home," he says. "Already, we have filters in libraries [required under the Child Internet Protection Act of 2001] blocking access to much of the Internet. Now we're talking about adding even more restrictions. It exaggerates the 'participation gap'—not a technology gap, but a difference in access to the defining cultural experiences that take place around technology today."

A Chilling Effect

Current Internet filters at schools and libraries—some aimed at pornography and obscene materials, some already targeting social-networking sites—have "a tremendous chilling effect on education," agrees Jeff Cooper, an educational-technology consultant and former high-school teacher in Portland, OR. "The 'Just Say No' philosophy has never worked," Cooper says. "You're lumping all social networking into the negative basket, and not giving kids any alternative. But there is so much good stuff online that nobody ever talks about."

Indeed, while it might be easy to agree that teens shouldn't be wasting time on MySpace or other social-networking sites while they're at school, DOPA would cover any site that allows networking and chatting. As one example, Cooper points to TappedIn.org, a social-networking and professional-development site for teachers. Students often use personal and public "rooms" on the site as part of virtual classroom activities. "It allows teachers to bring their students online in a very safe and secure environment," explains Cooper. "My concern isn't really that MySpace won't be accessible from schools, but that other sites like TappedIn will be banned."

FAST FACT

The American Library Association passed a resolution opposing the Deleting Online Predators Act at its July 2006 convention.

DOPA supporters frequently cite a 2000 report about online sexual victimization funded by the National Center for Missing and Exploited Children, which concluded that one-fifth of children have been sexually solicited in chat rooms, by instant message, or by e-mail. But in fact, as Boyd and other opponents point out, the same report states that most solicitations come from other young people—only 4 percent are from adults over 25—and that most kids deal with these solicitations simply by not answering or logging off. "To clamp down on a bunch of new networking sites really doesn't do anything" to stop sexual predators, says Cooper. "You might as well shut off the Internet entirely.". . .

In the longer term, predicts Boyd, the law would simply drive teen networking underground, where it would be more difficult for adults to monitor. "They'll be moving from site to site with a level of ephemerality that no one can keep up with," she says. "Not the cops— not even the designers of the technology."

EVALUATING THE AUTHOR'S ARGUMENTS:

The author argues that most questionable solicitations that teens receive from social networking sites come from other teenagers, not older predators. Does this fact, if true, weaken or strengthen the case for federal regulation of such sites? Defend your answer.

Social and Education Programs Can Prevent Child Abuse

"Investing more now in preventing child abuse and neglect . . . will save lives, reduce future crime and soon begin saving taxpayers' money."

Fight Crime: Invest in Kids

Fight Crime: Invest in Kids is a private anti-crime organization of law enforcement personnel, crime victims, and youth violence experts. In the following viewpoint, excerpted from a brief that focuses on child abuse in New York State, the authors state that child abuse in many high-risk families can be prevented by providing parents with education, training, substance-abuse treatment programs, and mental health services. Failure to provide such services is costly in the long run, both in terms of associated crime and in placing abused children in foster care, the authors conclude.

AS YOU READ, CONSIDER THE FOLLOWING QUESTIONS:
  1. What effect does child abuse have on future crime, according to the Fight Crime: Invest in Kids organization?

2. How effective in preventing child abuse are home visits by nurses who teach parenting skills, according to the authors?
3. How much money does child abuse and neglect cost America every year, according to the authors?

In New York, there were 74,483 officially recognized victims of child abuse or neglect and 71 confirmed deaths from abuse or neglect in 2004. In 2001, 14,800 children were removed from their homes. Even those tragic numbers, however, may mask the real toll of child abuse and neglect in New York. Nationally, the best estimate of the real number of children abused or neglected each year is closer to three times the official figure, and the Justice Department released a report saying deaths nationwide from abuse and neglect likely exceed 2,000 a year, instead of the 1,490 officially reported in 2004. So, the true number of New York children abused, neglected or even killed is likely to be much higher than the officially reported cases.

FAST FACT

According to the American Psychological Association, families that are socially isolated and who do not receive support from social services, kinship networks, or religious organizations are at higher risk for child abuse.

The Future Toll: 3,000 More Criminals

While most victims never become violent criminals, being severely abused or neglected can lead to permanent changes in children's brains. Some children have trouble learning empathy, while others develop a predisposition to misinterpret actions as threatening and react violently. This sharply increases the risk that these children will grow up to be arrested for a crime. The best available research indicates that, of the 74,483 New York children who were confirmed victims of abuse or neglect in 2004, approximately 3,000 will become violent criminals as adults who would otherwise avoid such crimes if not for the abuse or neglect they endured as children.

Preventing Abuse and Neglect

Failure to invest now in programs proven to prevent child abuse and neglect puts everyone in New York at greater risk of becoming a victim of crime. The more than 300 New York police chiefs, sheriffs, prosecutors, and crime victims who are members of Fight Crime: Invest in Kids call on their state and federal governments to:

Offer high quality coaching in parenting skills to all at-risk parents. The Nurse Family Partnership Program (NFP) randomly assigned at-risk mothers to receive home visits by nurses who provided coaching in parenting and other skills. Rigorous research originally published in the *Journal of the American Medical Association,* shows that children of mothers in the program had 48 percent fewer substantiated reports

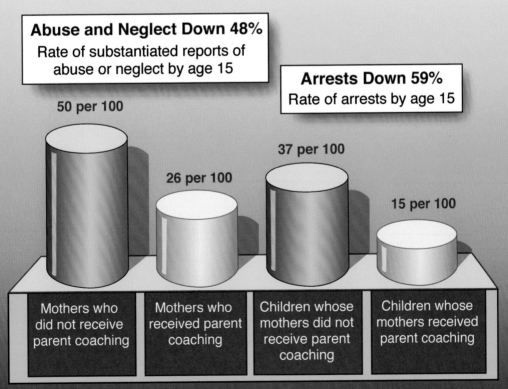

The Nurse Family Partnership Reduced Abuse Among At-Risk Kids

Abuse and Neglect Down 48%
Rate of substantiated reports of abuse or neglect by age 15

Arrests Down 59%
Rate of arrests by age 15

50 per 100

26 per 100

37 per 100

15 per 100

| Mothers who did not receive parent coaching | Mothers who received parent coaching | Children whose mothers did not receive parent coaching | Children whose mothers received parent coaching |

Source: "New Hope for Preventing Child Abuse and Neglect in New York: Proven Solutions to Save Lives and

of abuse or neglect. Put another way: in-home parent coaching services can prevent nearly half of all cases of abuse or neglect among at-risk children. In addition, by the time the children reached age 15, mothers in the program had 61 percent fewer arrests than the mothers left out of the program, and other children had 59 percent fewer arrests than the kids left out.

Offer quality pre-kindergarten programs with parent-training for at-risk children. The Child-Parent Center (CPC) preschool program serves Chicago families in low-income neighborhoods. Similar youth not receiving CPC were almost twice as likely to be placed in either foster care or adopted as the youth in CPC. Youngsters left out of CPC were also 70 percent more likely to have been arrested for a violent crime by age 18, and 24 percent more likely to be incarcerated as an adult than those receiving CPC.

Ensure that pregnant women who are addicted have access to drug and alcohol treatment programs. Maternal drug use during pregnancy can lead to brain damage in the child. Further, fetal alcohol syndrome is

Parenting classes have more influence over how today's families are run.

the leading cause of preventable mental retardation. The interaction of neurological damage at birth with deficient parenting multiplies the risk of criminality later in life. Research shows that an effective drug and alcohol treatment program for pregnant women in Baltimore dramatically reduced the number of babies who were born prematurely and at-risk for permanent brain damage that is associated with later criminality.

Provide mental health services for depressed or mentally ill parents. People who grew up with a household member who was depressed, mentally ill, or who attempted suicide were two times more likely to have been physically abused than those who did not grow up in such a household. Just like other ill parents, depressed or mentally ill parents can effectively raise children if they receive treatment. Yet studies show only 25 percent of individuals nationally who suffer from depression receive adequate care for their illness.

Saving Lives, Preventing Crime and Saving Money

Child abuse and neglect costs America upwards of $80 billion a year. Two-thirds of that is crime costs. In September, 2003 more than 37,000 New York children were in foster care. In 2004, $2.1 billion was spent on preventing or treating abuse or neglect in New York, including $706 million in state funding. Most of that went for providing necessary foster care and victim services, and that funding—while never adequate—must at least be maintained. Investing more now in preventing child abuse and neglect, instead of waiting to treat it, will save lives, reduce future crime and soon begin saving taxpayers' money. For example, the Washington State Institute for Public Policy found that nurse home visitation programs saved taxpayers and crime victims five dollars for each dollar invested. The Child-Parent Center preschool program saved taxpayers, victims, and participants ten dollars for every dollar invested (taxpayers alone saved almost $7).

Law Enforcement Leaders Are United

New York law enforcement leaders are calling for greater investments to protect children from abuse and neglect, save taxpayers' dollars, and make all New Yorkers safer. This call has been endorsed by the New York State Association of Chiefs of Police, the New York State Sheriffs' Association, and the New York State District Attorneys Association. The evidence is in. We can save millions of dollars in New York while preventing most abuse and neglect in high-risk families. The time to act is now.

EVALUATING THE AUTHOR'S ARGUMENTS:

The authors stress how preventing child abuse can save taxpayer money. Why do you think they focus on this argument?

Viewpoint
6

Better Parent-Child Communication Can Prevent Child Abuse

Jonel Aleccia

"Parents [should] . . . communicate with their kids, . . . [and] talk to them about good touching and bad touching."

Jonel Aleccia is a reporter for the *Spokesman-Review*, a newspaper in Spokane, Washington. In the following viewpoint, based on interviews with police detectives and other child abuse experts, she argues that parents must talk to their children about the differences between "good" and "bad" touching and how children have the right not to be made uncomfortable. Contrary to some public perceptions that the main child abuse threat comes from strangers, many child abuse perpetrators are trusted relatives or authority figures who cultivate relationships with children to the point where abuse victims do not know they are being abused, Aleccia writes.

AS YOU READ, CONSIDER THE FOLLOWING QUESTIONS:
1. What percentage of abused children are hurt by a parent, according to Aleccia?
2. How do child abusers gain the trust of their victims, according to the author?
3. Why is the problem of child abuse difficult to confront, according to Aleccia?

The thing is, the abuser was such a nice guy. He wasn't a monster, some stranger preying on the single mom and her 7-year-old daughter. He was a friend, a neighbor, a 35-year-old man who said he saw how hard the Spokane woman worked and wanted to help out. He carried her groceries. He bought her dinner. He offered to baby-sit.

And then, late at night, under the guise of watching TV, the nice guy molested the second-grader. "He started by rubbing her legs," said Detective Doug Orr, who conducts polygraph exams for the Spokane Police Department and the state Department of Corrections. "Then he penetrated her." The scary thing isn't just that such a scenario occurred, said Orr, who administered a maintenance polygraph . . . aimed at holding the convicted sex offender, now 42, to the terms of his probation. Equally alarming is how often it happens. "This is as routine as it gets," said Orr, who has interviewed hundreds of offenders in a two-decade career. While popular perception warns of "stranger danger" and urges society to protect children from outsiders, law enforcement experts and advocates for abused children say the real threat most often lurks close to home. Nearly 85 percent of abused children are hurt by a parent acting alone or with another person, according to the federal Child Welfare Information Gateway. That includes about 80 percent of sexual abuse cases and nearly 90 percent of neglect, and the ratio is as true in Eastern Washington and North Idaho as it is in the rest of the country. Perpetrators almost always are known to the victim, advocates say. Even worse, they're usually trusted relatives, friends or authority figures who use intimacy as a means for abuse.

"People who are worried about kids, about people on the playgrounds snatching them up, you're kind of misdirected," Orr said.

"I've only seen two or three of the 'bogeyman' type offenders in my career."

Abusers spend considerable time and energy getting close to their victims, a process known as "grooming," Orr said. That view is echoed by Marcia Black-Gallucci, an advocate with the Victims Rights Response Team, a Spokane agency that saw more than 9,000 clients last year. "If you're a trusting sort, the offender can groom the parent first," she said. "It can go on for a year or a long, long time." Serial abusers often reveal that they target vulnerable women with children, advocates said. "The really common scenario is a single mom whose boy friend is really good with her kids," Black-Gallucci said. "Afterwards, she says, 'He didn't value me, he didn't want me, he wanted access to my children.'" Other abusers seek out positions in which they'll have access to and authority over children. That can include coaches, teachers, youth group leaders and others. "Lots of Santa Clauses and clowns are molesters," Black-Gallucci said. Once they've gained trust, offenders slowly begin to display aberrant behavior. Physical abuse might begin with a shove, a slap or a harder-than-necessary spanking. Sexual abuse can start with affectionate back rubs or massages that gradually veer into private areas. "It starts with tickling over the clothing and then moves to tickling under the clothing," Orr said. Many offenders don't intend to hurt their victims, Orr said. They often claim to care about the children and tell themselves that the behavior wasn't wrong or that it wasn't as bad as it seemed.

"There's a lot of denial and minimization," Orr said. Offenders blur physical and psychological boundaries so thoroughly that victims often don't know they're being abused, experts said. They'll offer gifts, treats or special favors. They'll tell children that the abuse is OK, that it's normal, that everybody does it, Black-Gallucci said. "They'll tell the child: 'You and I are special. I love you in such a special, unique way.'" Physical abusers will tell their victims that they deserved the punishment, said Tinka Schaffer, an advocate at the Children's Village

FAST FACT

The majority of sexually abused children are victimized by family members or close friends, not by strangers.

Communication with positive adult figures could well be the key to keeping children safe from external dangers.

treatment center in Coeur d'Alene. "They'll say, 'I never hit you that hard; it was just a little swat,'" she said. The hardest thing about confronting abuse is cutting through the web of denial and distortion that surrounds it, experts said. The first step requires becoming aware that sexual, physical and emotional abuse exists. "We see it everywhere," said Black-Gallucci. "We walk down the street and say, 'You're an offender, I can just tell.'" That doesn't mean that people should become universally suspicious, Orr said. Even after two decades of analyzing sex offenders, he tells his children, ages 17, 15 and 11, that most people are good. "I tell my kids, that's only a small percent of the population," he said.

He urges parents to communicate with their kids, to talk to them about good touching and bad touching and why no one has a right to make them uncomfortable. "You don't have to worry about it, but you have to be concerned about it," Orr said. "And you have to sit down with your children and talk. End of book."

EVALUATING THE AUTHOR'S ARGUMENTS:

The intended audience of this article was primarily adults instead of children. Is there worthwhile information presented from a child's point of view, in your opinion? Why or why not?

Viewpoint
7

"Children are our most precious assets. . . . Let us not be afraid to intercede in their behalf if we observe abusive behavior toward them."

Observers Must Confront Abusive Parents to Stop Child Abuse

Ursula A. Falk

Ursula A. Falk is a psychotherapist. In the following viewpoint she describes disturbing instances of child maltreatment that she has witnessed. She argues that child abuse prevention is the responsibility of everyone, not just parents, and that people should not hesitate in confronting abusive parents or reporting them to the proper authorities.

AS YOU READ, CONSIDER THE FOLLOWING QUESTIONS:
1. What did Falk see at a picnic?
2. What did the author learn while working with disturbed young people at a mental health institution?
3. What do children learn from their parents, according to Falk?

Ursula A. Falk, "We Must Take a Stand Against Child Abuse," *The Buffalo News*, October 17, 2006, p. A8.

T wice in a month I witnessed incidents of children being abused by their parents.

While attending a picnic, I saw a developmentally young teenager dragged and severely punched in the shoulders and spine by a brutal father who had no patience with this unfortunate innocent human being, who played with the fervor that is normal for a child with his apparent handicap.

The young man writhed in pain and cried out in unintelligible animal-like howls, the only wordless tones he was able to utter. He was unable to wrest himself away from the fists of his merciless father, who added blows with his legs into the teen's body. It did not even stop when the boy was silent. The man threw his son into the car and after seemingly endless blows, locked the car door and walked away leaving the frail form of the bent-over child in the vehicle.

I was determined to report this incident to the Child Protection Agency but could not find the name of the perpetrator. A woman

Child abuse can take on many roles, such as this coach punishing young child athletes. Child abuse prevention must come not just from the parents, but also from other adult figures present in children's lives.

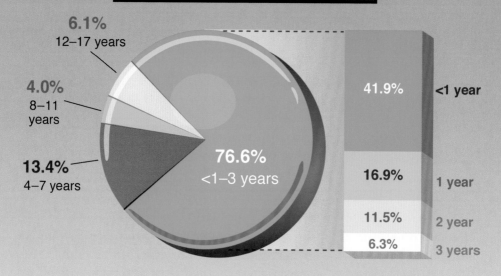

Age of Child Fatalities, 2005

6.1%
12–17 years

4.0%
8–11
years

13.4%
4–7 years

76.6%
<1–3 years

41.9% **<1 year**

16.9% **1 year**

11.5% **2 year**

6.3% **3 years**

Source: U.S. Department of Health and Human Services, Administration for Children and Families, *Child Maltreatment 2005* (Washington, DC: U.S. Government Printing Office, 2007).

who seemed to be the mother looked on in silence and did not move an inch, and kept on eating her food.

The Second Incident

The next incident occurred in the entranceway of a grocery store. The perpetrator was a large woman, apparently the mother of three sons. The older children seemed intimidated by her menacing voice. The youngest was between 3 and 4 years of age. He stepped out of a cart and stood in front of a candy machine. The screaming woman picked up the little boy and threw him forcefully back into the cart. Then with her raucous voice she redressed the other two young boys who were shaking with fright. She yelled that they were responsible for not paying closer attention to the little one so that she would not have to do so.

One of the bigger boys stood near her and looked beseechingly at this Amazon-like women lest he be the next victim of her wrath. She threatened that worse would await them when they got "home."

Child Abuse and Mental Illness

At one time, I worked in an institution for emotionally disturbed and delinquent children. Is it any wonder that these behaviors and mental illness are present in young ones who have seen adults act out in irrational, brutal and unloving ways? In my work with institutionalized young people, I found that those most affected have the tendency not merely to act out but become psychotic—they have a break in reality.

One example was a 7-year-old who walked around in circles and carried a sharp stick, swinging it continuously as he sang the following words in a dull repetitive monotone: "Beena, beena, beena, vooka." With the stick he was symbolically protecting himself against any onslaughts, and the words had meaning only to him.

Children learn kindness, caring and love from parents. How can children feel loving and loved when they see erratic and violent behavior from the grown-ups who are supposed to be there to love and protect them?

Criminologists and researchers in the field have found that 85 percent of adult prisoners who are incarcerated for violent crimes were raised in abusive homes. Behavior and attitudes are learned very early in children's lives.

FAST FACT

People in the following professions are required by law to report suspected child abuse or neglect to the authorities: doctors, dentists, mental health professionals, social workers, police, teachers, and child-care workers.

Our Most Precious Assets

Children are our most precious assets, they are our future and the future of our nation. Let us not be afraid to intercede in their behalf if we observe abusive behavior toward them.

EVALUATING THE AUTHOR'S ARGUMENTS:

Do the author's personal anecdotes and experience provide compelling arguments for her position? Why or why not?

Chapter 3

How Should the Government Deal with Child Abusers and Sex Offenders?

In 1992 U.S. Surgeon General Dr. Antonia Novello worked with lawmakers to make homes safer for children.

The Government Should Remove Child Abusers from Their Families

Maria Elena Salinas

"Some people are just not fit to be parents."

In the following viewpoint, syndicated columnist and Univision news anchor Maria Elena Salinas describes several horrific cases of child abuse. She argues that in too many cases warning signs regarding the parents were ignored by neighbors, social welfare agencies, and others. In some cases child welfare departments were investigating reported abuse but had not taken the children from their homes. She concludes that children should be promptly removed from their homes and placed into foster care or adoption in cases where mothers and fathers are abusive or neglectful.

AS YOU READ, CONSIDER THE FOLLOWING QUESTIONS:

1. What does Salinas find most alarming about the stories of child abuse she describes?
2. What cases of child abuse does the author describe?
3. What solution does Salinas suggest for children taken from abusive homes?

The squeaky noise emanating from a black plastic bag floating on the Pampulha Lagoon in the Brazilian town of Belo Horizonte caught the attention of a couple of villagers. They thought it was a cat meowing, and managed to pull the bag out of the water. To their surprise, it was not a screaming feline they found, but a 2-month-old baby girl.

How she ended up in the lake is still being investigated; the mother said she gave the baby away to some homeless people because she couldn't afford to keep her. Immediately, thousands of people offered to adopt the child. She was one of the lucky ones. At least she survived the ordeal.

There has been an alarming surge of stories in the news about children who have been neglected, abused, tortured or even killed. Yet even more alarming is the fact that in the majority of the cases, these children are victims of those who are not only supposed to be giving them love and attention but be protecting them from danger: adults, caretakers, their own parents.

Notorious Cases

Some of the most notorious cases have come out of the New York City area. Within a two-month period, five children died in their homes, among them 7-year-old Nixzmary Brown, who was allegedly beaten to death by her stepfather, Cesar Rodriguez, on Jan. 11 [2006] for eating a forbidden yogurt.

FAST FACT

In 2005 almost 3 percent of child fatalities in the United States happened to children who had been placed in foster care but were then returned to their biological families.

Like Nixzmary, dozens of kids have died at the hands of a stepfather or their mother's boyfriend, too often with the mother too weak to do anything to prevent it. Also in New York City, 4-year-old Quachon Brown died of fractures to the skull and severe lacerations to the liver. Allegedly, he was beaten by Jose Calderon, his mother's boyfriend, because he knocked down the TV set. In Indianapolis, 4-year-old Andrea Gonzales died of massive trauma to the head after

It is widely believed that children live happier lives once removed from their abusive natural home and placed in a foster home with caring adults.

her stepfather allegedly banged her head against the floor for having soiled her pants.

Two other cases of child abuse sent shockwaves through Nevada. In Las Vegas, police are still [in February 2006] trying to identify a little girl of Hispanic origin whose beaten body was found in a trash can. In nearby Carson City, a 16-year-old girl and her 11-year-old brother were kept locked in a bathroom. When they were discovered, she weighed 40 pounds, and her brother weighed 30; apparently neither had been to school for the past five years.

It was severe depression after learning that her husband wanted a divorce that apparently led Eleazar Paula Mendez to suffocate her three children in De Queen, Ark. She tried to kill herself by swallowing ant poison. She claims her children—an 8-year-old boy and 6-year-old twins—begged her to take their lives, too.

Of course, in her case there is no way anyone could have known that her despair would lead her to commit such an unspeakable crime. She has been described, even by her husband, as an extraordinary mother.

Living Arrangements of Child Abuse Victims, 2005

Victim Living With	Victim	
	Number	Percent
Married parents	40,770	11.1
Married parent and stepparent	4,210	1.1
Unmarried parents	10,583	2.9
Parent and cohabiting partner	9,567	2.6
Both parents, marital status unknown	49,103	13.4
Single parent, mother only	64,961	17.7
Single parent, father only	6,960	1.9
Single parent, mother and other adult	11,470	3.1
Single parent, father and other adult	1,283	0.3
Nonparental relative caregiver	8,792	2.4
Nonrelative caregiver	17,843	4.9
Group home or residential facility	1,985	0.5
Other setting	2,791	0.8
Unknown	84,750	23.1
Missing data	51,879	14.1
Total	**366,947**	**100.0**

This table, based on data from 28 states, shows the various living arrangements of child abuse victims.

Source: U.S. Department of Health and Human Services, Administration for Children and Families, *Child Maltreatment 2005* (Washington, DC: U.S. Government Printing Office, 2007).

But in too many cases, the warning signs are there and are ignored by other family members, social workers, school administrators and neighbors, who either don't take them seriously or don't want to get involved.

Reviewing Child Welfare Procedures

In New York City the rise in children's deaths has led authorities to take a close look into the effectiveness of the city's Children's Services, in all of the recent cases, the child-welfare agency had been investigating reports of abuse and neglect yet the children were left in a dangerous environment that eventually took their lives.

Within a week after the death of Nixzmary, the city's child-welfare office received more than 2,000 reports of abused children. At least 200 of them were taken away from their parents and put into foster care. The state Senate approved a bill that calls for a mandatory life sentence without parole for those who intentionally cause the death of a minor under 14. It's too late for five young victims.

Some People Are Not Fit to Be Parents

But even though the system failed these children, leaving them under the care of unfit parents or caretakers, it is not a bureaucrat who takes the life of a child. Some people are just not fit to be parents, and some single mothers are not mindful enough to put the safety of their kids above their love interests. There are thousands of responsible adults, many of whom cannot have children of their own, who can care for unwanted children through adoption. Somebody has to start minding the kids.

EVALUATING THE AUTHOR'S ARGUMENTS:

What guidelines if any does Salinas offer for determining exactly when social service agencies should take children away from their parents? Do you think more guidelines are necessary to accept her conclusion? Why or why not?

The Government Should Seek to Preserve and Help Troubled Families

Mike Arsham

Mike Arsham is a social worker and the executive director of the Child Welfare Organizing Project (CWOP), an organization that works to improve child welfare policies in New York City and to advocate for the rights and needs of biological parents. The following viewpoint was written shortly after the beating death of a seven-year-old girl, Nixzmary Brown, made headlines in New York and generated calls for reforming child protective services there. Arsham argues that the well-publicized death of Brown was creating a panic in the community that could lead to more children being summarily removed from families where abuse or neglect was suspected. He argues against such a policy, maintaining that his years of experience in social work have taught him that removing children and placing them in the foster care sys-

Mike Arsham, "Honoring Nixzmary's Memory by Avoiding a Panicked Response," *Gotham Gazette,* January 26, 2006. Reproduced by permission.

tem often does them more harm than good. Many, if not most, parents accused of child abuse are not criminals, states Arsham; instead, they are people struggling with poverty and other challenges. Furthermore, he contends, many parents are reluctant to seek necessary and available help from social services because of fears that they might lose their children.

AS YOU READ, CONSIDER THE FOLLOWING QUESTIONS:
1. What changes were made to New York's child welfare system in 1996, according to Arsham?
2. What contributions have birth parents made to the debate over protecting children from child abuse, according to Arsham?
3. What two opposing ideological views does the Administration for Children's Services reject, in the author's view?

Recently a brother and sister got into a scuffle at the office of the Child Welfare Organizing Project [in New York City] where I am the executive director. It was nothing serious, just play fighting. But the mother broke it up by saying, "God forbid that one of you get a mark on you and someone sees it!"

I work with parents who at one time or another have lost their children to foster care, and they are once again living with a fear that such families last felt a decade ago.

As soon as they, and I, saw the sensationalized press coverage about the death of seven-year-old Nixzmary Brown,[1] we were afraid the progress made in the last few years would unravel, due to subsequent political pressure.

A Policy of Removal

It was in January 1996, in the aftermath of the death the previous month of six-year-old Elisa Izquierdo, that the city reorganized and renamed the relevant city agency, calling it the Administration for Children's Services, and making as part of its mission statement the

---

1. Brown was found beaten to death on January 11, 2006, apparently by her mother's boyfriend.

Many believe that federal funding should go to private practice clinics that serve to help troubled families repair their shattered relationships.

policy that any ambiguity regarding a child's safety would be resolved by removing the child from his or her home.

In the two years following the new agency's inception, there was an increase of about 50 percent in the removal of children from their families. At the same time, since then-Mayor Rudy Giuliani believed that overzealous efforts to preserve families contributed to Elisa's death, he slashed preventive services by 18 percent. Preventive services are anything provided to a family to help make it unnecessary to remove a child, such as housing, food stamps or day care.

Child neglect became criminalized during that time. Low-income mothers were arrested and prosecuted for offenses that were basically the result of being poor—such as leaving their child alone while they worked in a sweat shop or living in "substandard housing" that was actually city housing.

Having worked in preventive services and seeing firsthand how much it can accomplish, I believe that many of the parents who had children removed in the 1990's could have had it handled in a way that would better serve the long-term interest of their children.

Of course, none of us at the Child Welfare Organizing Project felt that parents who mistreat their children should be molly-coddled, and I'm not saying that parents whose kids were removed back then were totally blameless. Many needed help and many made mistakes. Some who had substance abuse issues truly were not in a place where they could take care of their children.

Oversimplifying the Issue

But we also felt that the Administration for Children's Services was oversimplifying the issue. We knew that families caught up in the system were much more complex than the way they were being handled. And reflexively removing children tends to weaken and destroy the bonds in families that are fragile to begin with. It permanently undermines the parents' authority and the children's faith in their parents' ability to protect them. And many of the children who have been in care for any length of time have experienced abuse in their foster homes, often far in excess of what their parents were accused of.

We invited those parents to share their experiences. Theirs was a perspective to which nobody had paid attention. Eventually they were speaking to professionals in the child welfare system and in other venues where their voices had previously not been heard. The child welfare system became aware that birth parents were not criminals, but complicated people leading challenging lives, often struggling with issues related to being poor.

> ## FAST FACT
>
> Several states, including Michigan, Minnesota, Missouri, and North Carolina, have adopted "dual track" responses to reports of child abuse, with less serious cases of neglect being handled by family support services rather than criminal prosecution.

Maltreatment Experiences of Children While in Foster Care

Type of Maltreatment	Percent of Foster Children Affected
Some child mistreatment	32.8 percent
Physical neglect only	10.1 percent
Physical neglect and physical abuse	9.4 percent
Physical abuse only	5.6 percent
Sexual abuse and other maltreatment	4.0 percent
Sexual abuse only	3.7 percent

Source: National Center for Youth Law, *Youth Law News*, July–September 2005.

Things began to change in the direction for which we at the Child Welfare Organizing Project had hoped. The Administration for Children's Services became less ideologically driven—subscribing neither to the ideology of "when in doubt, remove the child," or the equally extreme "preserve families at all costs." It moved closer to taking into account the actual individual needs of specific children and their families.

The number of kids going into foster care decreased and the city reinvested in preventive services. The number of kids known to the Administration for Children's Services who died annually did not increase, as some feared it would. But now the fear is that all the publicity and public outcry around Nixzmary is bringing us back to the time where a birth parent was an object of suspicion, and all the progress made is in danger of being lost.

Fear Among Birth Parents

The birth parents who work at CWOP are also afraid on a much more visceral level. They know that once a parent has had a kid in foster care, that parent is much more likely to lose that kid again, because of that history.

Since Nixzmary's death, whenever a school teacher or guidance counselor calls a parent at CWOP, and I hand the phone to them, I see their hearts leaping to their throats. They're wondering what has happened that could have resulted in a call to ACS.

There are definite signs that a panic like the one a decade ago is underway. There is reportedly a 30 percent increase in protective removals already this month [January 2006] so far, compared to January 2005. Meanwhile, our phone at CWOP hasn't stopped ringing. We are trying to ride out this media frenzy and use it to make the points we want made. . . .

We believe that the best way to honor Nixzmary's memory is not by going back to a time when the Administration for Children's Services was just one more threat to family life in poor communities, but by continuing to change the system for the better.

EVALUATING THE AUTHORS' ARGUMENTS:

Both Arsham and Maria Elena Salinas make the killing of Nixzmary Brown a central part of their arguments. How do their assessments of that case and its ramifications differ? Do you agree or disagree with their views of how that particular case can and should affect the debate over government policies on child abuse? Defend your answer.

Child Predators Need Both Punishment and Treatment

Jake Goldenflame

"[The law should] confine the offender in prison until he is healed, and see that he gets an opportunity to be healed: that would be wisdom, which we have a right to demand of the law."

Jake Goldenflame is a journalist, lawyer, and author. He is also a convicted child sexual abuser who works with sex offenders and who advocates for programs to treat them. In the following viewpoint, excerpted from his book *Overcoming Sexual Terrorism*, Goldenflame argues that efforts to rehabilitate sex offenders are more effective when they focus on helping them control their impulses rather than curing them. He criticizes laws against sex offenders as being overly punitive and counterproductive to the goal of reducing child sexual abuse. Goldenflame acknowledges that some studies show that sex offenders who have received therapy reoffend at the same rate as those who have not had therapy, but he states that it is unjust to deny sex offenders the opportunity to turn their lives around. He suggests that some sex offenders may benefit from a spiritual component added to their treatment.

AS YOU READ, CONSIDER THE FOLLOWING QUESTIONS:

1. What treatments of sex offenders have failed in the past, according to Goldenflame?
2. What argument does the author make comparing sex abuse impulses to diseases like diabetes and AIDS?
3. What prevents many imprisoned sex offenders from confessing past offenses in therapy, in the view of the author?

Treatment for sex offenders is not a new art. In the early part of the twentieth century, neurosurgeons simply cut out that part of the person's brain that had to do with the sex drive. According to Canadian sex therapist W.L. Marshall, one of the pioneers of newer treatments, a group of German surgeons were the leading advocates of that earlier method. When they later found that the number of patients who committed new sex crimes following surgery was still no lower than that of those who had been spared the surgeon's knife, the human brain as the sole location of our sex drive was dropped, along with that form of therapy.

Surgical castration was popular for awhile in Europe, and at first looked like it promised success as many patients went back to the community and remained arrest-free. But then someone noticed that the patients included a number of homosexuals, who hadn't raped women or molested children in the first place, which presumably accounted for why they weren't "repeating" those crimes now. When they were removed from the follow-up statistics, early optimism quickly faded as the readjusted figures showed that almost half of all the remaining sex offenders who had been castrated still continued to masturbate or have intercourse, something anyone who knew history could have told them:

> It had been known from Greek times, and probably before, that castration did not eliminate sexual desire and that a castrate who had preserved his penis was, under certain circumstances, capable of having erections . . . and could even be aroused to a kind of ejaculation. . . . [Reay Tannahill, *Sex in History*]

It should not have been surprising, then, that while a 1968 study indicated that Danish castrates did stop committing any more sex crimes, a third of their number continued to commit other crimes, which suggested that their underlying aggression hadn't been changed. And when hormones became commercially available, permitting a patient to cancel the effect of castration, there seemed no point to continue using this method to control offenders and it was discarded.

Psychologists didn't do much better when they applied conventional therapy. One California program for sex offenders had a 19 percent failure rate among its patients over a three-year follow-up period. When it was extended to five years, the re-offense rate jumped to 26 percent and the program became politically unsupportable. The problem, it was later learned, was that therapists were seeking the wrong goal: trying to *cure* a problem that would be more successfully addressed if it was just placed under control. As [Janice K. Marquez in the California] mental health department put it:

> ... There appears to be an emerging consensus among treatment providers . . . that the overall goal of treatment is one of management or control, not cure. This rejects the notion that sex offending is an *illness* from which one will recover and that successful treatment will result in the elimination of the disorder. Instead, it suggests that successful interventions are those that train offenders to reduce exposure to situations that place them at risk for reoffense. . . .

A lot of things can't be "cured." No cures exist for AIDS, diabetes, schizophrenia and numerous other medical and psychiatric conditions. But they can be controlled so that the individual afflicted with them can continue to live in the community without endangering himself or anyone else. In spite of the sometimes sensationalistic reporting given to the most extreme (and, fortunately, rare) cases, recent statistics show that many sex offenders can be taught how to manage their own behavior. The author, for example, is in his fifteenth year of remaining free from re-offending at the time of this writing.

When a new pilot program designed to pursue *self-control* instead of cure was carefully tried out by the State of California, the re-offense rate for its graduates was reduced by two-thirds. Sex offending might

Special Commitment Centers give sex offenders the chance to receive treatment, as well as to be kept away from the victims they would prey upon.

not be curable, but it could be controlled—for the rest of the former offender's life—by the offender.

Barriers to Treatment

Treatment doesn't begin until we're ready to really face ourselves. And if you are a sex offender in a time when the climate all around the subject has been shaped primarily by the victims of sexual offenses, facing yourself may be very hard to do. Victims, quite naturally, choose to utterly demonize sex offenders and they have enormous political influence.

The result . . . is that many of our treatment programs have been hobbled by laws that don't mean to heal anybody, but only seek vengeance.

Obviously if, as their sponsors believe, punishment really is the answer, there wouldn't be a sex offender anywhere in the world today. Over the last twenty years, punishment has so reshaped criminal law that penalties have been raised to the skies, yet sex offenders continue to exist and their crimes continue to be as awful as before. The fact that sex offenders are fewer in number only means that punishment has done as much as it can but it has not eliminated the problem.

Punishment alone, therefore, is not the answer. But it is part of the answer. I know of no better place to put a convicted sex offender than in prison for, like a monastic cell, it leaves him alone with his problems so that he finally has no choice but to face them. . . .

To Heal or to Punish?

When my request for further psychotherapy was approved, I was given a prison psychologist with whom I'd meet each Monday for one hour. To prepare for those sessions, I had the guards lock me in my cell the day beforehand, so I could have the time and the privacy to search within myself for anything I wanted to bring up.

I was amazed to find so many injuries buried in my memories: like the fact that my father had rejected me as a child because I didn't like football or baseball like he did. I liked swimming and, when I got into my teens, I'd even begun working-out at a gym, but those activities weren't good enough to earn his acceptance. That hurt me, even then.

Then there was my mother, and all those times when she'd kept me from being me by denying that I felt whatever I felt if it differed at all from how she felt. What I soon realized was that, like all sex offenders, I'd never really had any sense of self—of being a person whose faith in himself, alone, was adequate to meet the challenges that life presents.

Lacking that, I had no self-respect and, without self-respect, no respect for anyone else. So I lived a life that disrespected me, I traveled in its gutters instead of in its heavens, unconsciously believing that I didn't deserve the heavens because I'd never been treated as someone who did.

The lesson that leaves us with is that, if you want your child to become a moral person, you begin by respecting him or her as a person: as a human being possessed with whatever their unique talents might be. You encourage the genius given to them by their nature. You don't try to make your child into your reflection but into their own.

Fear of Confession in Therapy

I told my doctor that the reason I wanted to see him was because I wanted to learn why I had molested my daughter. Fearful that I might be prosecuted further if I said anything about any other acts I had committed, I did what everyone else did in prison and never mentioned them. Had I done otherwise, they would have been reported and I might have had to face additional charges.

Some say that not talking about them is harmful, as it doesn't get all of the person's problems addressed. In a case handed down in the United States just before the time of this writing (*McKune v. Lile*), the Supreme Court said much the same thing. Under its ruling, states were given permission to make a prisoner's confinement even harsher if he wouldn't tell his keepers about crimes for which he had not yet been caught. But doctors I know who conduct group therapy programs outside of prison, which often include men still awaiting trial—men who can't talk about their crimes, on the advice of their attorneys, say that such men are still dealing with their problems just by being in the group. "They hear what we're saying and they know if it applies to them."

Perhaps what the defense bar still hasn't succeeded in communicating to the bench is that, unlike tent revival meetings, where a sinner cannot be forgiven unless he loudly proclaims all his sins to others, psychotherapy is a different kind of process altogether. What is necessary in psychotherapy is that you face the truth about yourself, to yourself. It is the individual who has to do the work, not the doctor. Whether the patient tells the doctor about something or not, the patient still knows what that something is and is working on it, even when confining the discussion only to those things which can safely be discussed.

As I wrote, in part, to [Linda Greenhouse,] the *New York Times* reporter who covered that United States Supreme Court case:

> For all the importance that an honest admission has, speaking out of my own experience I say that it doesn't necessarily have to be made to a person who will prosecute you for it. . . . There are those who, as in *Lile*, believe . . . one can only find redemption by self-rejection, while there are others . . . who believe one can only find redemption by accepting one's self as their life does: as a work still in progress, and then progressing it.

Who is going to risk being given another prison sentence when they haven't even finished the one they already have, just to fill in the record?

Evil or Ill?

To meet this challenge, some prosecutors are now choosing not to press charges for disclosures made by prisoners in prison therapy programs. They are issuing what are called waivers from further prosecution for anything admitted in counseling, and that is helping a lot of men to get the help they need without having to fear more jail time for doing so.

The only problem is that further criminal prosecution isn't the only threat that an admitted offender now faces in some states. Since at least the early nineties in the United States, new laws now require some sex offenders to be committed to mental hospitals after their imprisonment if they admit too much, keeping them locked up even longer. As a result, some defense attorneys are warning their clients that freedom from criminal prosecution isn't enough and, so far as this writer knows, no prosecutor yet has waived both further prosecution and post-imprisonment civil commitment, moving us right back to where we started: offenders—fearful of no end to being kept locked up—are not willing to divulge any other crimes than the ones for which they've been convicted.

And some won't even choose to see a doctor out of fear they would be prosecuted for saying anything.

This nation needs to make a choice as to whether we are evil or ill. If evil, and no more than that, prison alone, for life, is all that is called for. But if driven to do evil by forces we never chose, you get the person treated so he can have his life back. To punish a person for having mental problems hasn't been done since the Dark Ages.

The point is made best by one of the letters I received from convicted sex offenders all over my nation. It came from a person who raped his three-year-old brother; one of the worst crimes it is possible to imagine.

But he is only fourteen years old and hasn't a clue as to why he did this. Can we possibly be so barbaric that we would say punishment alone is all he needs?

Are we so lacking in charity for a child driven by evil forces to do a deed like this that we will not help him get his mental health back? If we, as a people, cannot see those who obviously need treatment as deserving of the same, then we are spiritually ill, for we have lost our connection to the human heart.

Blame and Responsibility

My doctor was no fool, by the way. He was a prison psychologist, accustomed to facing men who lied to him every day. I doubt that I really had to tell him there might have been other offenses. As a result, by the end of a year of our meeting together, he had some answers for me.

"While it's clear that your father never molested you, there's no question but that he was, shall we say, 'overly-affectionate.' And that it was your mother who was the problem."

I recall that the doctor said I should hate her "as she was the one who messed you up."

He wasn't the first doctor who had said so. While I was in treatment and my case was waiting to be heard, another doctor had said the same thing.

But as I told this doctor, I just didn't think that hating my mother was the answer.

"I know too much about her own background to do that. That she damaged me I do not doubt. But that she alone did so is untrue as she, in turn, had been damaged

by those who raised her who, in turn, had been damaged by others, and so on, making it merely an act of choice to say we shall blame her, as if none of these others had ever existed. All of them molested me."

Blame is just a legal term, used by courts to determine who is going to pay the injured party, in cash or through involuntary servitude as a prisoner of the state. It has nothing to do with healing, where we can identify the source of the damage so that it can be removed.

Other people who look like the creator of the damage are only carriers of a damaging process that moves through them. While they can—and should—be held accountable for letting it come through, we can't accurately call anyone its real creator because there is no such individual. There is just life, and in life sometimes people get hurt: earthquakes happen and people get injured by them. Emotional earthquakes happen, too, and that's what sometimes makes a parent fail. You can't blame anyone for having an emotional earthquake. The best you can do is build them back up so they don't have another.

In that respect, the view expressed by our criminal law—that the offender, alone, is to blame for having become an offender—is like blaming a storm on itself, without including the climate that produced it. In the victim's pain, he or she wants vengeance, and who can fault them? All he can see is the offender himself, not all of the others who may go back for generations in the forming of that offender. And so the victim cries out of his pain, "Punish him!"

But law should have more vision than that and, instead of merely punishing, it should also seek to confine the offender in prison until he is healed, and see that he gets an opportunity to be healed: that would be wisdom, which we have a right to demand of the law.

The doctor stared at me in wonder, and with a wry grin on his face said, "You're crazy, did you know that? You're as crazy as Charles Manson."

Seeking Spiritual Healing

I wanted additional answers, so the following week I sent in a request for something called transpersonal counseling, which would look not only at my mind but into my spirit itself. I now suspected that my spirit had been damaged, too, and needed to be fixed if I was ever to have a life that was under my control. When I received a reply that this kind of counseling wasn't available in any of the prison's psychology programs I turned, instead, to where it could be found: in the Chaplain's Office.

Statistical findings since that time may suggest that I was wise to do so as it now turns out that offenders who have had therapy do no better than those who had none. Comparing members of both groups it was found that, after twelve years, one out of every five men in both groups re-offends. Those who do and do not receive therapy do just as well.

EVALUATING THE AUTHOR'S ARGUMENTS:

Does the personal experience of Jake Goldenflame make his arguments on rehabilitating child predators more or less credible, in your view? Explain.

Viewpoint 4

Child Predators Should Be Executed

Dave Gibson

> *"[The death penalty] is not only a just punishment, but the most effective way to prevent more children from becoming victims."*

In the following viewpoint, Dave Gibson tells the sad case of a child who was kidnapped, raped, and murdered by a person who had been previously convicted of child molestation a few years earlier. Gibson argues that society is not doing enough to protect children from child predators who either go uncaught or leave prison (after serving their sentences) as dangerous as ever. It is impossible to "cure" or rehabilitate child sexual predators, Gibson argues. He calls for the death penalty as the only just punishment that would also prevent additional children from becoming victims. Gibson is a political consultant and a columnist.

AS YOU READ, CONSIDER THE FOLLOWING QUESTIONS:
1. How many times was John Couey arrested before he murdered Jessica Lunsford, according to Gibson?
2. What percentage of children suffer some form of sexual abuse or assault, according to the author?
3. What percentage of child molestation cases are reported to the authorities, according to Gibson?

Dave Gibson, "Killing Child Molesters Should Be as Socially Acceptable as Killing Nazis," *The American Daily*, March 28, 2005. Reproduced by permission.

Six decades ago, it was difficult to find any civilized person who did not see the Nazis as pure evil. Those same civilized people accepted the only way to deal with Hitler and his henchmen was to kill them. While the Nazis terrorized Europe and murdered and enslaved Jews (and anyone else deemed "unworthy") child molesters are perpetrating another type of holocaust, on the children of America. Their brand of evil can be dealt with in only one fashion . . . Death!

Failing to Protect the Innocent

The [2005] abduction and murder of nine year-old Jessica Lunsford by convicted child molester John Couey, is just the latest glaring reason to extend the death penalty to child molesters. The notion that child molesters can be somehow rehabilitated is nothing more than a wishful thought from bleeding-heart liberals. While the leftists bend over backwards to defend the most evil amongst us—children continue to be robbed of their innocence and in some cases their lives.

46-year-old John Couey lived a mere 150 yards from the Lunsford home. This predator entered the home in the dark of night, kidnapped

A makeshift dungeon used to hold teenage girls against their will led to the legal ruling in South Carolina that allows the death penalty for sex offenders convicted of raping children younger than eleven years old.

Jessica, raped her, murdered her, and then buried her tiny body in a shallow grave. Among his 24 arrests over the last 30 years, Couey was arrested and convicted of molesting a young girl in 1991. Jessica was not only the victim of an evil human being, she was in fact the victim of a justice system which fails to protect the innocent.

According to the National Center for Missing and Exploited Children, 20 percent of all U.S. girls and 10 percent of all U.S. boys suffer some form of sexual assault, before reaching adulthood. Child molestation is a national epidemic.

Why Rehabilitation Efforts Fail

The California Department of Corrections reports that over half of convicted sex-offenders return to prison, within a year of their

release. That number jumps to three-fourths, after a year. In fact, 20 percent of all U.S. prison inmates report to having molested a child. State prisons typically attempt to isolate convicted molesters from the general population, to prevent savage beatings and worse . . . (even armed robbers and murderers find child molesters to be repugnant). However, incarceration does nothing to end their desire to abuse children. You simply cannot punish the evil "out of someone"—you can only extinguish that evil.

According to the National Institutes of Health, the average child molester sexually abuses 117 children over his lifetime. When you consider all of the relationships that child will have (parents, siblings, grandparents, friends, spouse, their own children)—the number of lives affected by such a damaging event is astounding.

We currently deal with the molester with incarceration and so-called "rehabilitation." Once that molester is released, most states require that he registers himself as a sex-offender. There are currently [2005] more than 400,000 registered sex-offenders in the United States. This tactic too has proven useless. California for instance, recently reported that they cannot account for the whereabouts of 33,000 of their registered offenders.

When one considers that the crime of child molestation is an incredibly under-reported crime, the evil that this nation's children face is overwhelming. According to the FBI, less than 10 percent of molestations are ever reported.

Ridding the Nation of Child Predators

We are simply failing to protect our kids.

Many Europeans found it easier to simply turn away, as the Nazis massacred the Jews. They found it easy, that is, until their own loved-

States Allowing Death Penalty for Rape

This map shows the U.S. states that have authorized capital punishment in cases of nonhomicidal child rape.

States allowing death penalty for child rape

ones were in danger. We can no longer turn a blind eye to the hordes of child molesters preying upon our children. If we do not protect the most vulnerable amongst us . . . we deserve all of the suffering which this life can offer.

It is time to demand from our legislators and our courts, that those who rob children of their innocence be put to death. It is not only a just punishment, but the most effective way to prevent more children from becoming victims.

Let us rid this nation of child molesters, the way we rid the world of Nazis. If our legislators and judges lack the courage to do so . . . then they can consider themselves just as the guilty as the predators they protect!

EVALUATING THE AUTHOR'S ARGUMENTS:

The author compares child predators to the German Nazis who perpetrated the Holocaust during World War II, calling both "pure evil." Do you believe such comparisons (and labels) oversimplify the situation, or do they provide a needed perspective to the debate over how society should treat child abusers? Defend your answer.

Facts About Child Abuse

The Prevalence of Child Abuse

- Roughly 3 million cases of child abuse or neglect are reported each year, of which roughly 1 million are substantiated.
- A report of child abuse is made every ten seconds.
- More than fourteen hundred children die annually from inflicted injuries.
- Seventy-five percent of child homicide victims are under fourteen years old.
- Forty-five percent of child homicide victims are under twelve months old.
- Child abuse is one of the leading causes of injury-related mortality in children.
- Sixty percent of reported child abuse cases are about child neglect—the failure to provide for a child's basic physical and mental needs.
- An abused child has approximately a 50 percent chance of being abused again.
- According to the Community Coalition Against Family Violence, 75 percent of child abuse cases go unreported.
- The National Center for Missing and Exploited Children estimates that one in five girls and one in ten boys will be sexually exploited before they reach adulthood.
- Of sexual abuse cases of children under twelve, 90 percent of the victims knew the perpetrator.

The Consequences of Child Abuse

According to Childhelp, a national nonprofit organization dedicated to helping victims of child abuse and neglect:

- Sexually abused children are 2.5 times more likely to abuse alcohol and 3.8 times more likely to become addicted to drugs.
- About 30 percent of abused children become abusive parents, compared to 2 to 3 percent of all individuals.

- In the United States 36.7 percent of women in prison and 14.4 percent of men in prison were victims of abuse as children.
- By age twenty-one 80 percent of young adults who had been abused as children meet the diagnostic criteria for at least one psychiatric disorder, such as depression or post-traumatic stress syndrome.
- Abused children are 25 percent more likely to experience teen pregnancy.
- Child abuse victims are 59 percent more likely to be arrested as a juvenile.

Reporting and Responding to Child Abuse

According to *Child Maltreatment, 2005,* a report of the U.S. Department of Health and Human Services, Administration for Children and Families:

- Approximately 3.3 million allegations of child abuse and neglect involving 6 million children were made to child protective service (CPS) agencies in fiscal year 2005.
- About 62 percent of those allegations reached the report stage and either were investigated or received an alternative response.
- In 28.5 percent of the investigations that reached the report stage, it was determined that at least one child was a victim of child abuse or neglect.
- Only .1 percent of child abuse reports investigated in 2005 were ruled to be intentionally false.
- The average time for CPS agencies to respond to child abuse allegations was eighty-nine hours, or approximately four days.
- The average number of child abuse cases completed per investigative worker in 2005 was 67.5.
- The three most common sources of child mistreatment reports in 2005 were from teachers, police officers, and social service staff.
- The three largest groups of nonprofessional reporters were anonymous (9.0%), "other" sources (8.1%), and relatives (7.9%).

Child Abuse and the Law

- Federal law defines child abuse as any recent act or failure to act on the part of a parent or caretaker that results in death, serious physical or emotional harm, sexual abuse or exploitation; or an act or failure to act that presents an imminent risk of serious harm.

- State laws establish definitions of what exactly constitutes child abuse and neglect. Although all states must comply with the basic standards set by federal law, different states have varying definitions of child abuse.

- State laws require most professionals, including teachers, lawyers, social services staff, doctors, police officers, day-care workers, and foster care providers, to notify CPS agencies of suspected child mistreatment.

- Criminal statutes define child maltreatment that is punishable through the criminal justice system. Forms of child abuse criminally punishable include homicide, murder, manslaughter, false imprisonment, assault, battery, criminal neglect and abandonment, child prostitution, computer crimes, rape, deviant sexual assault, indecent exposure, and reckless endangerment.

- Juvenile court jurisdiction statutes provide definitions of the circumstances necessary for the court to have jurisdiction over a child and to allow for the child's removal from the home or to order treatment services for the parents. They determine minimum standards of care and protection for children.

Organizations to Contact

The editors have compiled the following list of organizations concerned with the issues debated in this book. The descriptions are derived from materials provided by the organizations. All have publications or information available for interested readers. The list was compiled on the date of publication of the present volume; the information provided here may change. Be aware that many organizations take several weeks or longer to respond to inquiries, so allow as much time as possible.

American Bar Association Center on Children and the Law
40 15th St., NW, Washington, DC 20005
(202) 662-1720
Web site: www.abanet.org/child
The Center on Children and the Law is a program of the American Bar Association that provides information about children's legal rights and child protection laws.

American Humane Association Office of Public Policy
206 N. Washington St., Suite 300, Alexandria, VA 22314
(703) 836-7387
e-mail: publicpolicy@americanhumane.org
Web site: www.americanhumane.org
The American Humane Association works to protect both children and animals from willful abuse and neglect. It conducts research, maintains a database of official reports of child abuse and neglect, and publishes numerous pamphlets and books.

American Professional Society on the Abuse of Children (APSAC)
PO Box 30669, Charleston, SC 29417
(843) 704-2905
e-mail: apsac@comcast.net
Web site: www.apsac.org
APSAC provides education and information to professionals who work in child abuse research, treatment, prevention, and related fields. It publishes the *Journal of Interpersonal Violence.*

Childhelp USA
15757 N. 78th St., Scottsdale, AZ 85260
(480) 922-8212
Web site: www.childhelp.org
Childhelp USA is a nonprofit organization dedicated to meeting the needs of abused and neglected children. Its programs include a hotline (1-800-422-4453) open twenty-four hours a day that children can call with complete anonymity. It also promotes public awareness of child abuse issues and publishes the book *Child Abuse and You.*

Children's Healthcare Is a Legal Duty, Inc. (CHILD)
Box 2604, Sioux City, IA 51106
(712) 948-3500
e-mail: childinc@netins.net
Web site: www.childrenshealthcare.org
CHILD is a nonprofit organization that is dedicated to protecting children from religious- and cultural-based abuse and medical neglect. CHILD publishes a newsletter and has news releases available on its Web site.

False Memory Syndrome Foundation
1955 Locust St., Philadelphia, PA 19103-5766
(215) 940-1040
e-mail: mail@fmsfonline.org
Web site: www.fmsfonline.org
The False Memory Syndrome Foundation believes that many "delayed memories" of sexual abuse are the result of false memory syndrome (FMS). In FMS, patients in therapy "recall" childhood abuse that never occurred. The foundation publishes a newsletter and various papers and distributes articles and information on its Web site.

International Society for Prevention of Child Abuse and Neglect
245 W. Roosevelt Rd., Bldg. 6, Suite 39, West Chicago, IL 60185
(630) 876-6913
e-mail: ispcan@ispcan.org
Web site: www.ispcan.org
The International Society for Prevention of Child Abuse and Neglect, founded in 1977, is the only multidisciplinary international organization that brings together a worldwide cross-section of committed professionals to work toward the prevention and treatment of child

abuse, neglect, and exploitation globally. Its primary publication is *Child Abuse and Neglect: The International Journal.*

Justice for Children
2600 Southwest Fwy., Suite 806, Houston, TX 77098
(713) 225-4357
Web site: www.justiceforchildren.org

Justice for Children is a national nonprofit organization of citizens concerned about children's rights and their protection from abuse. It opposes family reunification policies that may endanger children.

Kempe Center for the Prevention and Treatment of Child Abuse and Neglect
1825 Marion St., Denver, CO 80218
(303) 864-5300
e-mail: questions@kempe.org
Web site: www.kempecenter.org

The center provides clinically based educational resources for training, consultation, program development and evaluation, and research in child abuse and neglect.

National Center for Missing and Exploited Children (NCMEC)
Charles B. Wang International Children's Building
699 Prince St., Alexandria, VA 22314
(703) 274-3900
Web site: www.missingkids.com

The NCMEC works to prevent child abduction and sexual exploitation and to assist child victims of these crimes, their families, and professionals who serve them. It provides information on child sexual abuse on its Web site.

National Center for Prosecution of Child Abuse
99 Canal Center Plaza, Suite 510, Alexandria, VA 22314
(703) 549-4253
Web site: www.ndaa-apri.org/apri/programs/ncpca/ncpca_home.html

The center seeks to improve the investigation and prosecution of child abuse cases. It provides updated information on child abuse laws and court reforms and supports research on reducing courtroom trauma for child victims.

National Coalition for Child Protection Reform
53 Skyhill Rd., Suite 202, Alexandria, VA 22314
(703) 212-2006
Web site: www.nccpr.org

The NCCPR is a group of professionals and others who believe that many efforts to take children away from their families are counterproductive, and it works to change policies concerning child abuse, foster care, and family preservation. Its publications include issue papers on child abuse, orphanages, and foster care.

National Council on Child Abuse and Family Violence (NCCAFV)
1025 Connecticut Ave. NW, Suite 100, Washington, DC 20026
(202) 429-6695
e-mail: info@nccafv.org
Web site: www.nccafv.org

The NCCAFV works to oppose all forms of intergenerational violence, including child abuse, by providing public education materials, resource development consultation, and technical assistance to government and social agencies.

Prevent Child Abuse America
200 S. Michigan Ave., 17th Fl., Chicago, IL 60604
(312) 663-3520
Web site: www.preventchildabuse.org

Prevent Child Abuse America is a national organization dedicated to developing public policies that strengthen families and prevent child abuse. Its reports, fact sheets, and press releases may be viewed on its Web site.

PROTECT: National Association to Protect Children
46 Haywood St., Suite 315, Asheville, NC 28801
(818) 350-9350
e-mail: info@protect.org
Web site: www.protect.org

PROTECT is a national membership organization that lobbies for changes in laws to punish child abusers and protect children from child abuse. Articles and information on its political strategies are available on its Web site.

For Further Reading

Books

Chris Becket, *Child Protection: An Introduction.* Thousand Oaks, CA: Sage, 2007. A comprehensive textbook for social work professionals and others interested in protecting children from child abuse.

Bette L. Bottoms et al., *Ending Child Abuse: New Efforts in Prevention, Investigation, and Training.* Binghamton, NY: Haworth, 2006. A collection of articles by professors and social work professionals.

Isobel Brown, *Domestic Crime.* Broomall, PA: Mason Crest, 2003. A sourcebook on child abuse and other forms of domestic abuse for younger readers.

Nick Bryant, *The Franklin Scandal: A Story of Powerbrokers, Child Abuse, and Betrayal.* Walterville, OR: Trine Day, 2008. An investigate journalist delves into a nationwide child-trafficking and pedophilia ring in the United States.

Robin E. Clark et al., *The Encyclopedia of Child Abuse.* Rev. ed. New York: Facts On File, 2007. This comprehensive reference work has more than five hundred entries as well as statistical information and bibliographies.

Stephen Dean, *Sexual Predators: How to Recognize Them on the Internet and on the Street. How to Keep Your Kids Away.* Lansdowne, PA: Silver Lake, 2007. A television journalist provides practical advice and information to parents and children about child abusers who use computers to approach their victims.

Melissa J. Doak, *Child Abuse and Domestic Violence.* Detroit: Thomson Gale, 2007. A reference book that provides statistical and other information on the social problem of child abuse.

Linda Lee Foltz, *Kids Helping Kids: Breaking the Silence of Sexual Abuse.* Pittsburgh: Lighthouse Pointe, 2003. An examination of child sexual abuse that features first-person narratives of victims and their struggles for recovery.

Richard J. Gelles, *The Book of David: How Preserving Families Can Endanger Children's Lives.* New York: Basic, 2007. An examination of one tragic case of child murder that calls into question the social welfare goal of keeping families together.

John Haley and Wendy Stein, *The Truth About Abuse*. New York: Facts On File, 2005. An "A-to-Z" reference that provides basic information about all forms of domestic abuse.

Chris Hansen, *To Catch a Predator: Protecting Your Kids from Online Enemies Already in Your Home*. New York: Dutton, 2007. Hansen, a *Dateline* reporter noted for his sting operations against child predators, examines the problem and how families can protect themselves.

Myra L. Hidalgo, *Sexual Abuse and the Culture of Catholicism: How Priests and Nuns Become Perpetrators*. Binghamton, NY: Haworth Maltreatment and Trauma, 2007. A child abuse survivor and mental health practitioner examines the child sex abuse scandal within the Roman Catholic Church.

Eileen Munro, *Effective Child Protection*. Thousand Oaks, CA: Sage, 2003. A book for professionals in child welfare and abuse prevention that uses case studies to examine how to make decisions in the best interests of the child.

John E.B. Myers, *Child Protection in America: Past, Present, and Future*. New York: Oxford University Press, 2006. A history of how American communities sought to protect children from abuse from colonial times to the present.

Deanna S. Pledge, *When Something Feels Wrong: A Survival Guide About Abuse for Young People*. Minneapolis: Free Spirit, 2003. A book that provides checklists, journaling ideas, and other positive ways of dealing with physical, sexual, or emotional abuse and how victims can and should seek help.

Periodicals

Peter Aldhous, "Sex Offenders: Throwing Away the Key," *New Scientist*, February 21, 2007.

Sarah Childress, "Fighting over the Kids; Battered Spouses Take Aim at a Controversial Custody Strategy," *Newsweek*, September 25, 2006.

Ta-Nehisi Paul Coates, "When Parents Are the Threat," *Time*, May 8, 2006.

Richard Cohen, "Deterring Common Sense," *Washington Post*, January 24, 2006.

Juvenile Justice Digest, "Wisconsin Adopts New Policy for Child Abuse," June 16, 2006.

Katy Kelly, "To Protect the Innocent," *U.S. News & World Report*, June 13, 2005.

Kelly Colleen McDonald, "Child Abuse: Approach and Management," *American Family Physician*, January 15, 2007.

John F. McManus, "Childless Politician Wants to Ban Spanking," *New American*, February 19, 2007.

Daryl T. Moore, "Breaking the Cane: A Child-Abuse Survivor Reclaims His Mother's Love Years After Enduring Cruel Beatings at the Hands of His Stepfather-Brothers," *Essence*, April 2003.

Joan Morris, "For the Children: Accounting for Careers in Child Protective Services," *Journal of Sociology and Social Welfare*, June 2005.

L. Martin Nussbaum, "Changing the Rules: Selective Justice for Catholic Institutions," *America*, May 15, 2006.

Pamela Paul, "Is Spanking O.K.?" *Time*, May 15, 2006.

James Poniewozik, "Breaking America's Favorite Taboo," *Time*, October 16, 2006.

Maia Ridberg, "A Push to Focus on Worst Cases in Child Abuse," *Christian Science Monitor*, January 26, 2006.

Carol Rust, "Yates: A New Insanity Angle," *Newsweek*, March 13, 2006.

Hani Salehi-Had et al., "Findings in Older Children with Abusive Head Injury: Does Shaken-Child Syndrome Exist?" *Journal of the American Academy of Child and Adolescent Psychiatry*, December 2006.

Julie Scelfie, "Taboo: Spanking Smackdown," *Newsweek*, February 5, 2007.

Kathy Sena, "Still Haunted by What Could Have Happened," *Newsweek*, February 13, 2006.

Andrea Seymour, "Knowledge Is Power: The Ability to Accurately Track Children in Care Can Keep Them Safe," *Policy and Practice*, March 2007.

Jim Shields, "Family Violence and the War in Iraq," *Houston Chronicle*, March 24, 2007.

Nathan Thornburgh, "The Kidnapper's Trick," *Time*, September 18, 2006.

Matthew Trokel et al., "Variation in the Diagnosis of Child Abuse in Severely Injured Infants," *Journal of the American Academy of Child and Adolescent Psychiatry*, January 2007.

Cathy Young, "Parent Trap," *Reason*, December 2006.

Web Sites

Child Abuse—MSN Encarta (http://encarta.msn.com/encyclopedia_761562624/Child_Abuse.html). The entry on child abuse from Microsoft's Encarta encyclopedia.

Child Abuse: Statistics, Research, and Resources (www.jimhopper.com/abstats/). Created by a child abuse researcher and instructor at Harvard Medical School, this Web site has statistics on child abuse in the United States, Canada, Great Britain, and Australia as well as information on how to think critically about these statistics and how they are derived.

Child Welfare Information Gateway (www.childwelfare.org). Formerly the National Clearinghouse on Child Abuse and Neglect, this Web site, maintained by the Children's Bureau of the Department of Health and Human Services, provides access to information and resources about child abuse in order to help protect children and strengthen families.

Netsmartz Workshop (www.netsmartz.org). A Web site providing information on how to keep young people safe from internet victimization.

Our Kids: Our Business (www.spokesmanreview.com/ourkids). A special section of the *Spokesman-Review* Web site containing articles, multimedia content, Internet discussions, and other resources in recognition of Child Abuse Awareness Month 2007.

The Zero—The Official Website of Andrew Vachss (www.vachss.com). Contains articles and information about the famed author and lawyer who specializes in representing abused children.

Index